The Time-Life Gardener's Guide

TREES

A

BOOK

Other Publications:

MYSTERIES OF THE UNKNOWN
TIME FRAME
FIX IT YOURSELF
FITNESS, HEALTH & NUTRITION
SUCCESSFUL PARENTING
HEALTHY HOME COOKING
UNDERSTANDING COMPUTERS
LIBRARY OF NATIONS
THE ENCHANTED WORLD
THE KODAK LIBRARY OF CREATIVE PHOTOGRAPHY
GREAT MEALS IN MINUTES
THE CIVIL WAR
PLANET EARTH
COLLECTOR'S LIBRARY OF THE CIVIL WAR
THE EPIC OF FLIGHT
THE GOOD COOK
WORLD WAR II
HOME REPAIR AND IMPROVEMENT
THE OLD WEST

For information on and a full description of any of
the Time-Life Books series listed above, please call 1-800-621-7026
or write:

    Reader Information
    Time-Life Customer Service
    P.O. Box C-32068
    Richmond, Virginia 23261-2068

This book is one of a series of guides to good gardening.

The Time-Life Gardener's Guide

TREES

TIME-LIFE BOOKS, ALEXANDRIA, VIRGINIA

CONTENTS

1

PLANTING YOUR TREES

2

CARING FOR TREES

3

PRUNING TREES

hether you choose them for the seasonal color provided by flowers, fruits and leaves, or for the unchanging beauty of evergreens, the trees you have will dominate your garden. They form the living architecture of the landscape; they shape its space in three dimensions—and they do so over long spans of time. It therefore pays, both economically and in subtler satisfactions, to choose them with forethought, plant (or transplant) them with care and maintain them faithfully.

This volume describes the sizes and shapes in which trees grow, the forms in which nurseries and mail-order houses make them available, and the professionals' techniques for planting, maintaining and propagating them. At the end of the volume is an illustrated dictionary of trees, in which you will find descriptions of more than 100 selected species and varieties, together with the zones in which they flourish best and the soil and climatic conditions they need.

1
PLANTING
YOUR TREES

P lanting is the first step in getting trees off to a good start. It must be done in timely fashion, in a well-chosen and well-prepared site, and with good stock. On the following pages you will find information about planting techniques: digging a hole that will allow the roots room to spread; how to prepare, maneuver and secure the tree when you plant it; tips on choosing new trees; how to site them to best advantage for sun and shade and in respect to other plantings in your garden; how to dig up a tree and move it if you are transplanting one you already have.

In buying a new tree, it is best to deal with a reputable nursery or mail-order house and to buy the best tree of its kind you can find. Think not only about appearance, but about the nature of the tree itself. Trees do best in areas to which they are indigenous; taking a tree out of its accustomed environment—planting a Douglas fir accustomed to the frigid climate of Maine, for example, in the warm sun and desert sand of Arizona—will decrease its chances of survival, so check zone information before buying. If you buy from a local nursery or garden center, the chances are that the stock is local, but if you buy from a distant mail-order house, be sure to check the zones in which a given tree flourishes before buying it (see the Zone Map on pages 84-85 and the Dictionary of Trees on pages 96-137). No matter what the environment, trees transplant most successfully when they are young, unstaked and have straight, slightly tapered trunks. When you see one you like, flex the trunk; it should bend easily and then return upright—a sign that it will be able to withstand wind as it is establishing itself in your garden.

For most trees, the ideal time to plant is autumn. As air temperatures cool, growth in the top of the tree slows down. But all through the fall and up until the ground freezes in winter, the soil remains warm and the roots can grow without having to compete with weeds for water. By the following spring, the tree will have a good root system to support the season's new growth and help the tree withstand the summer's heat, and will be ready to reward you with years of enduring beauty.

A CONTAINER-GROWN TREE
WITH NEATLY PACKAGED ROOTS

Its swirling branches dressed in yellow-green spring foliage, a honey locust thrives on a sunny lawn. Honey locusts grow fast and are often started in containers.

Tree farms and plant nurseries often grow and sell their stock in containers because, with the roots neatly packaged, such trees are easy to handle and transport. This means that containerized saplings are readily available. They are also somewhat easier to plant than trees that come with their roots wrapped in burlap *(page 12)* or bare-root *(page 14)*. But it also means that the buyer has to look out for some special danger signs.

The principal risk is that a tree may have become too old and large for its container. The result will be overcrowded roots, with major ones twining around and choking one another. Healthy young trees will have fairly dense root balls. But ones showing pretzel-like contortions, especially of the major roots, should be avoided. Ask the nursery assistant to remove at least part of the root ball from its container and check for excessive compaction and crowding.

Check at the same time to see that the soil around the roots is moist and mostly weed-free; dust-dry earth and weeds indicate neglect. And beware of yellowing, brittle leaves or needles, a sure indication of inadequate water or nourishment or both.

Removing root balls from the various sorts of containers tree growers use is simple. Roots slip fairly easily from plastic containers *(opposite)*. Paper-mache pots need only to be peeled off. A pot made of peat can be planted along with the roots, since it will decompose in the ground; all you have to do is slice off the bottom and the upper rim of the pot. Metal containers, though, tend to stick to the roots and often require cutting with heavy shears, a job that can be done at the nursery. When planting the tree, make sure to dig a hole that is as deep as the root ball and twice as wide.

1 Dig a hole that is about twice the diameter of the root ball and just as deep. To remove a young tree from a plastic container, place the container on its side, tap it a few times to loosen the root ball and then gently slip the container off the root ball. Do not pull on the trunk or the branches; wrenching can injure the tree. In general, move and lift the tree as much as possible by the root ball and handle its upper parts sparingly.

2 If the root ball is compacted and has some circling roots, you will need to do some minor cutting. Using a knife or a sharp trowel, make a slit 1 or 2 inches deep in the root ball's sides and bottom —down one side, across the bottom and up the other side. The severed roots will send out new shoots that will grow straight. You should also cut off any dangling roots that are broken or damaged.

3 Place the tree in the hole. Set it so that the bottom of the trunk will be flush with the soil. To test its position, lay a straight length of wood across the top of the hole. The topmost roots should be flush with the wood. Correct the depth if necessary by digging to lower the tree or shoveling soil into the bottom of the hole to raise it.

4 Using a shovel, fill the area around the roots with the soil you dug up when making the hole. It is a good idea to have mixed some fertilizer into the soil before pouring it back; a handful or two of the all-purpose fertilizer called 5-10-10 will do. Elaborate enriching of the soil with mulch or other organic materials, however, is not recommended. As you pour in the fill, firm the soil with your hands to eliminate air pockets.

5 When the root ball is covered, make a shallow water basin from excess fill, firming up a circular earthen rim about where the outside of the root ball would be. A new tree needs plenty of water and the small levee will concentrate it on the roots. Then cover the fill with shredded tree bark or other mulch, which will help conserve moisture and keep the soil from becoming too hot or too cold.

6 Turn on your hose so that it produces a slow trickle. Place the hose end inside the basin you have made around the tree. Let it run for 30 minutes for a good deep soaking. Repeat this a couple of times during the first week after planting. Thereafter give the tree another deep soaking once a week during the tree's first two or three years. □

A FIELD-GROWN TREE WITH ROOTS WRAPPED IN BURLAP

Buying a young tree that has its roots covered with soil and wrapped in burlap will probably be somewhat more expensive than purchasing either a bare-root tree or one grown in a container. (For one thing, it costs the tree grower time and effort to ball up the roots.) But there are distinct advantages. Such trees are generally larger than the other sorts, and may be more vigorous, since they have grown naturally in a field and have good fresh earth packed around the roots. Another advantage is that planting them, as illustrated here, is particularly easy.

But there can of course be problems, and it is wise to examine the tree. First of all, the burlap itself needs looking at. More than one layer of wrapping may mean the tree was dug up so long ago that the original burlap began to fall apart. Such a tree has remained in the nursery too long. Similarly, roots growing through the burlap indicate the tree has been out of the ground for weeks. Avoid it and look for something fresher.

Then there is the root ball inside the burlap. It should be solid and the earth should be moist. Dry, crumbly soil indicates insufficient watering—and probably poor overall care. So does yellow, dry foliage.

Once bought, a balled-and-burlapped tree should be planted as quickly as possible. The sooner it is back in the earth soaking up nutrients the better. Should you have to delay planting, keep the root ball wrapped and well watered. As with all trees, it should be planted in a hole twice as wide as (but no deeper than) the root system.

A sturdy, symmetrical pine, planted in a front yard, offers both beauty and a measure of privacy. Pines and most other evergreens are frequently sold with their full root systems wrapped in burlap.

1 Dig a hole twice the width of the root ball and just as deep. Use your hands to maneuver the wrapped root ball into its hole. If the tree is too heavy to lift easily, roll the ball into position. To adjust the tree so that the best side faces correctly, rotate it at the root ball, not the trunk.

2 Loosen the burlap; cut any strings and remove any staples or nails that bind it. If the burlap is natural untreated fiber that will disintegrate in the earth, fold the burlap back into the hole as shown above. Do not leave any aboveground; it will act as a wick and draw moisture from the soil into the air. If the burlap has been treated with a preservative, you will need to remove it. Rock the root ball back and forth, pulling on the burlap, until the whole wrapping comes free.

3 Mix the earth taken from the hole with a handful or two of all-purpose fertilizer; then backfill around the root ball. As you fill, tamp the soil three or four times to eliminate any air pockets. After the hole has been filled up, make a water basin and then cover the area with mulch, as shown on page 11. Water slowly but thoroughly. □

A BARE-ROOT TREE FOR EASY HANDLING

Most young trees sold in the condition called bare-root come from mail-order houses. There are good reasons to buy from such firms. They offer wider selections of species than local nurseries, their prices are often lower and the reputable mail-order firms generally sell excellent stock.

Still, anything bought sight unseen needs careful inspection—especially, in this case, the roots. They should spread in all directions and should show no mildew or fungus and little or no damage. A few breaks here and there are to be expected and can be trimmed *(below),* but major wounds will cause the tree to grow poorly. Any tree with battered or diseased roots should be returned.

Another possible pitfall is getting a tree that is unsuited to the environment. Nurseries usually stock only species that will thrive in their area, but mail-order firms have been known to ship southern magnolias to Minnesota or blue spruces to Mississippi. To make sure a tree can survive in your climate, consult the Dictionary of Trees *(pages 96-137).*

Finally, bare-root trees should arrive in a dormant state because they must be planted that way in late fall or early spring, so the roots can grow before the top awakes. Late autumn is preferable except for needle-leaved evergreens, which require a lot of water to become established and do best when planted during the damp spring months. In either case, a bare-root tree should be planted promptly. If bad weather prevents planting the day the tree arrives, store it in a cool, sheltered place and cover the roots with a damp cloth or wet newspaper.

A crabapple adds its garlands of white to a garden's joyous bursts of spring color. Such decorative trees are often sold bare-root by mail order.

1 Dig a hole having a diameter that is as wide as the spread of the roots. Remove the packing material carefully—the roots of any dormant plant are brittle—and inspect the tree for disease and abnormal breakage. Trim off any broken or twisted root tips with garden clippers *(right).*

After doing the trimming, place the tree's roots in a bucket of water and let them soak for about an hour. This initial drink will give the tree a reserve of moisture it can use after being planted.

3 Set the tree in its hole; with one hand support the trunk and with the other spread the roots *(left)*. Be sure the top roots are flush with the ground. Backfill with fertilized soil, working it around the roots and tamping it down to eliminate air pockets.

4 Make a water basin around your tree at the rim of the planting hole. Then water with a slow-trickling hose for only about 15 minutes; the loose soil around the bare roots will absorb moisture quickly and over-watering can promote disease. Repeat the brief watering two or three times a week until the ground freezes and the roots go dormant for the winter. □

ALL ABOUT TREES
AND HOW TO USE THEM

*Used as a decorative planting in front of a home,
a Canary Island date palm sends out a fountain
of rich green swordlike leaves. Date palms, which
grow as high as 50 feet, are tropical evergreens
that flourish only in the warm sun of Florida and
other semitropical parts of the United States.*

Trees are by all odds the most important elements in the landscaping around a house. Handsome plantings of trees add beauty and elegance—and cash value—to any property. They offer cool, inviting shade during the hot months and can deflect the wind when winter comes. Their flowers, buds and berries provide splashes of color. Used as screens, trees give privacy and block out eyesores. Their leaves even cleanse the air of pollutants.

To grow well and look effective, trees have to be carefully chosen, and planted in the right spots. Even a handsome tree planted in the wrong location may become an unsightly annoyance. Imagine putting a young maple in a small front yard —and finding that the grown tree dwarfs the lot, hides the front door and casts the house in deep gloom during the brightest days of summer. A handy rule: do not buy a tree and then decide where to put it. Rather, study a spot and match the tree to it. The landscape plan on the facing page shows some ideal places to plant and suggests some first-rate choices of trees.

Happily, trees come in a vast variety of shapes and sizes *(pages 18-19),* and so they offer a wealth of options. The many deciduous trees have special virtues, providing shade in summer, brilliant color in the fall—and bare branches in winter that let in the sun. Tall evergreens make fine windbreaks and screens, keeping their color year round; small ones make neat accents around windows and doors.

There is rich variety as well in the colors and textures of bark, of foliage, of flowers and fruits and pods *(pages 20-21).* Choosing trees that offer such extra interest can produce not just a handsome setting for a house, but what amounts to a garden in the air full of contrasts, surprises and delights.

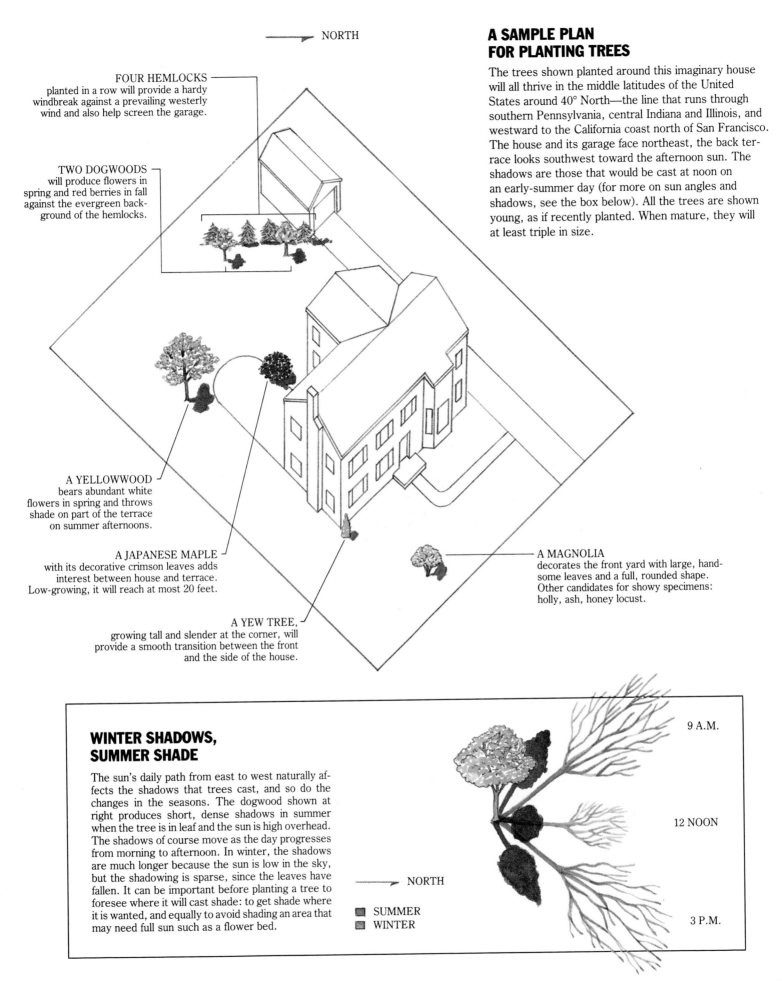

NORTH

FOUR HEMLOCKS
planted in a row will provide a hardy windbreak against a prevailing westerly wind and also help screen the garage.

TWO DOGWOODS
will produce flowers in spring and red berries in fall against the evergreen background of the hemlocks.

A YELLOWWOOD
bears abundant white flowers in spring and throws shade on part of the terrace on summer afternoons.

A JAPANESE MAPLE
with its decorative crimson leaves adds interest between house and terrace. Low-growing, it will reach at most 20 feet.

A YEW TREE,
growing tall and slender at the corner, will provide a smooth transition between the front and the side of the house.

A SAMPLE PLAN FOR PLANTING TREES

The trees shown planted around this imaginary house will all thrive in the middle latitudes of the United States around 40° North—the line that runs through southern Pennsylvania, central Indiana and Illinois, and westward to the California coast north of San Francisco. The house and its garage face northeast, the back terrace looks southwest toward the afternoon sun. The shadows are those that would be cast at noon on an early-summer day (for more on sun angles and shadows, see the box below). All the trees are shown young, as if recently planted. When mature, they will at least triple in size.

A MAGNOLIA
decorates the front yard with large, handsome leaves and a full, rounded shape. Other candidates for showy specimens: holly, ash, honey locust.

WINTER SHADOWS, SUMMER SHADE

The sun's daily path from east to west naturally affects the shadows that trees cast, and so do the changes in the seasons. The dogwood shown at right produces short, dense shadows in summer when the tree is in leaf and the sun is high overhead. The shadows of course move as the day progresses from morning to afternoon. In winter, the shadows are much longer because the sun is low in the sky, but the shadowing is sparse, since the leaves have fallen. It can be important before planting a tree to foresee where it will cast shade: to get shade where it is wanted, and equally to avoid shading an area that may need full sun such as a flower bed.

NORTH

■ SUMMER
■ WINTER

9 A.M.

12 NOON

3 P.M.

PYRAMIDAL
Norway Spruce
80 feet high

FULL-CROWNED
Red Oak
80 feet high

FOUNTAIN
Royal Palm
60 feet high

A WIDE VARIETY OF TREE SHAPES

When choosing a young tree to plant, it helps greatly to visualize what it will look like when grown—how broad, how narrow, how large-crowned and above all how tall. A towering tree can simply overpower a small lot; a short, stumpy tree can look silly in a wide-open space. The drawings below show seven basic tree shapes, ranging from the stately pyramid of a Norway spruce to the plump roundness of a full moon maple. Few of these trees will be nearly so tall as indicated here when you buy them in a nursery. When purchasing a tree, however, it is helpful to know how tall it may grow and how fast. Some trees grow very swiftly—willows and sweet gums, for example—and are useful if shade is wanted fast. Others such as oaks grow extremely slowly.

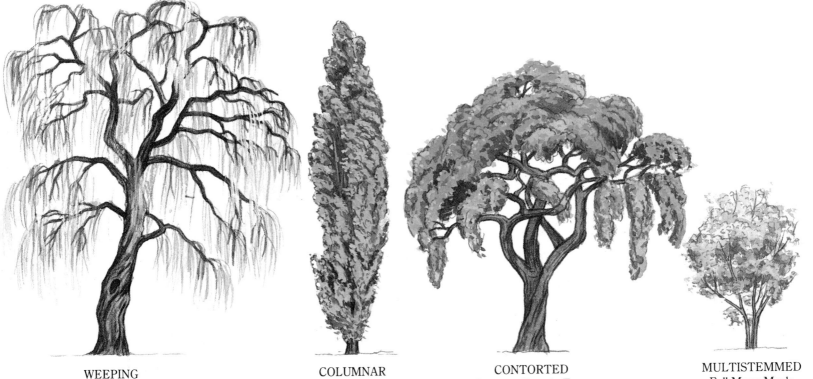

WEEPING
Golden Weeping Willow
50 feet high

COLUMNAR
Lombardy Poplar
50 feet high

CONTORTED
Japanese Pagoda Tree
40 feet high

MULTISTEMMED
Full Moon Maple
20 feet high

AMUR CHOKECHERRY

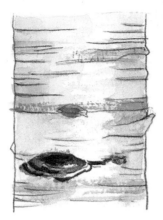

YELLOW BIRCH

MADRONE

MANY-TEXTURED AND COLORFUL BARK

Bark is an integral part of a tree's beauty and character, and should be taken into account when choosing what species to plant. In texture it may be ringed and glossy, as on an Amur chokecherry, or ringed and rough-textured like raw silk, as in yellow birch, or peeling, as in madrone. The color may be a luminous white, silvery gray, any of several yellows, reds or browns, or near black.

COMPOUND-LEAVED WILLOW

SIMPLE-LEAVED MAPLE
(Spring and Autumn)

NEEDLE-LEAVED EVERGREEN PINE

THE VERSATILE VARIETIES OF LEAVES

Tree foliage may be simple-leaved, compound-leaved or needle-leaved. Simple-leaved trees—oaks, maples and the like—produce the brightest green canopies and the densest shade in summer, and generally the brightest crimsons and golds in fall. Compound-leaved trees, such as willows, look more delicate and provide dappled shade, a benefit for neighboring plants that need some sun. Needle-leaved trees usually stay green all year, providing color when other trees are bare.

FLOWERING
DOGWOOD

TREE BLOSSOMS: BRIEF BUT BRILLIANT

Flowering trees add an extra lovely dimension to a landscape. Most bloom only in the spring and their flowers do not last long, but while decked in their finery they are among the most heart-lifting sights in nature. Among the splashiest blooms are those of the magnolia; others, such as silk tree and red maple flowers, have an airy delicacy. And some trees, like dogwood and crabapple, stage an encore, producing bright berries or attractive fruits later in the season.

SILK TREE

SOUTHERN
MAGNOLIA

RED MAPLE

SWEET CRABAPPLE

NUTS, BERRIES AND OTHER BONUSES

Many sorts of trees put forth large cones, shiny nuts, bright red berries or other decorative seed-carrying fruits and pods such as those shown here. Besides offering extra color and variety—often in the fall when it is especially welcome—such seed producers attract birds and other interesting, welcome wildlife. A bit of caution though: a tree that drops large cones or pods can be a nuisance if it overhangs a walkway or a terrace, and may clutter up the pavement. Such trees are better situated at the border of a woodsy area. □

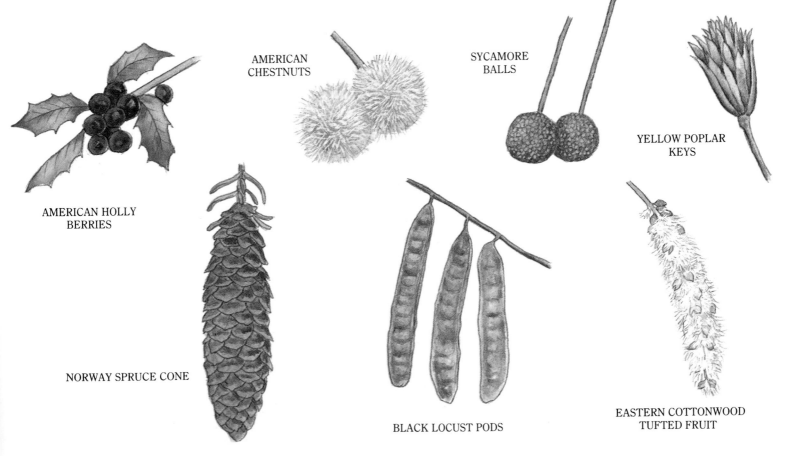

AMERICAN
CHESTNUTS

SYCAMORE
BALLS

YELLOW POPLAR
KEYS

AMERICAN HOLLY
BERRIES

NORWAY SPRUCE CONE

BLACK LOCUST PODS

EASTERN COTTONWOOD
TUFTED FRUIT

TRANSPLANTING A SMALL DECIDUOUS TREE

There are a number of reasons why even a small tree may need to be dug up and moved. Perhaps it is getting too big for its site or is casting too much shade in the wrong place. Or maybe it will be needed in another spot to provide shade. A large tree should be moved by a professional. But a small one—up to 6 feet tall and having a trunk no more than 1 inch in diameter—can be moved by any gardener with a strong back.

Whatever the reason for moving, the essence of transplanting a tree is the same as planting a new one: the root ball must be kept intact and prevented from drying out. The illustrations below and at right show how to get the roots of a small deciduous tree out of the ground and moved without injuring them.

Evergreens, which have heavier tops and therefore larger root balls, are best wrapped in burlap for transplanting (pages 24-27). For digging the hole and replanting, see the general instructions on pages 14-15.

Besides moving the root ball safely, the key to successful transplanting is timing. The optimum seasons, as with a new bare-root sapling, are late fall and early spring, when the tree is dormant. Having shed its leaves, a deciduous tree is lighter and easier to handle. Far more important, the roots survive the move more easily. Not required to send large amounts of moisture to leafy branches during dormancy, the roots suffer less "water stress." Never transplant during the warm months; disturbed roots are highly vulnerable to drought and heat.

The large heart-shaped leaves of a diminutive princess tree cast a dappled shade on the lawn beneath it. Princess trees are among those that can be transplanted bare-root when they are young.

1 To dig up a tree for transplanting, use a spading fork. Dig in a circle at least 12 inches from the trunk *(right)*. Push the tines deeply into the ground, then ease down on the handle to lift earth and roots together *(far right)*. Continue going around until the tree is loose.

2 Once the root ball is free, lift the tree from the ground, supporting its weight by putting one hand underneath the root ball. If the tree is too heavy to lift easily by hand, slip a board into the hole and underneath the roots to lever them upward. Hold the base of the trunk only to keep the tree upright. Do not lift by the trunk; doing so may injure the connections between the trunk and the top roots.

3 Brush off any excess dangling clods with your hand to lighten the load and make moving easier. But leave most of the soil clinging to the root ball. The fine fibrous roots will continue to draw moisture from the soil, lessening the stress of the move.

4 To shift the tree to its new location, lift the root ball onto a piece of burlap, cotton or plastic. Pull the material up around the roots *(left)*. Drag the tree to the edge of its fresh hole and replant immediately. The roots should be exposed to sun and wind as briefly as possible. Water gently *(page 11)*. □

MOVING A TREE
IN A BURLAP SQUARE

The tried-and-true way to transplant a tree with a substantial root system is to borrow a trick from tree farmers: wrap the roots in a good-sized square of burlap. Provided you choose a tree with a trunk no bigger than 1 inch in diameter (bigger than that will be too heavy), no large problems are involved. The main requirements—illustrated on these pages—are to free the root ball from the earth without harming it, and to get the burlap under and around it.

This sort of transplanting has several advantages. First, the burlap wrapping helps keep the bulky root ball and its earth in one solid piece. The burlap also helps protect any bruised or exposed root tips from wind and sun while the tree is being moved, lessening water loss (and thus stress) to the tree. Further, a well-wrapped root ball can be maneuvered easily into its new location.

As with the other planting and replanting operations described in this chapter, the best seasons to do the digging and moving are late fall and early spring, that is, when the tree is dormant. An evergreen, although it will not shed all its foliage in autumn and winter, transpires less moisture during the cool months. The roots thus retain more moisture, which helps them get reestablished. In very cold regions spring is probably preferable, because it spares the fresh transplant winter's punishing weather

The best time to transplant is when the ground is moist but not waterlogged. Moist soil will cling to the roots. Sodden ground is too heavy to work.

Laden with spring blooms, the boughs of a small cherry tree arch gracefully toward the lawn. Such trees, when young, are easily moved with the aid of a burlap sheet.

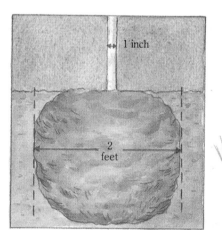

1 With a curved-blade shovel, dig a circular trench around the tree you are moving. The radius of the circle should be 1 foot for every inch of the trunk's diameter *(inset)*. A 1-inch-thick trunk requires the trench to extend at least 12 inches distant from the trunk on all sides.

2 After the trench is as deep as it is wide—here 24 inches—use a spade to shave the sides of the ball of earth until you reach the roots. (There is no point in lifting the weight of extra moist soil.) Work carefully and do not chop at the ball; you can easily injure the delicate outer root tips.

3 Place the spade under the shaved root ball, then push it with your foot as shown. Go to the other side of the tree and repeat the process. The idea is to lift the root system from the ground gradually. You may sever the bottom end of the taproot, but it will grow again.

4 Tip the tree over on one side. Place a sheet of burlap in the bottom of the hole, pushing one side under the root ball as far as possible *(above, left)*. Then tip the tree to the other side and draw the burlap under the roots and up around the root ball *(above)*.

5 Before trying to lift the tree, pull the sheet of burlap around the root ball and secure it by knotting the diagonally opposed corners. The burlap itself should be biodegradable —that is, made of natural fibers untreated with any chemicals—so that the wrapping can be left on the lower part of the root ball when you replant *(pages 12-13)*.

6 If the tree is light enough to be moved handily, lift it out of the hole and drag it to its new location by grasping the burlap's tied corners. It should be replanted without delay and watered slowly but generously with a hose. For trees heavy enough to put undue strain on the burlap or your back, try the modest bit of soil engineering shown below. □

RAISING A TREE FROM ITS TRENCH

To elevate a heavy tree from a hole in the ground, push the tree onto its side and shovel some of the soil you dug from the hole against the burlapped roots. After you have formed a mound, tip the tree in the other direction and onto the mound. Add more dirt on the other side of the roots. Repeat those steps, alternating from side to side, until the root ball sits at ground level. Roll the root ball onto a large cloth and drag it to its destination.

2
CARING FOR TREES

Compared with other showpieces in your garden, trees may seem relatively self-sufficient, the kind of plants you can put in the ground and forget about. After all, in a forest they propagate themselves and survive on their own. But if they are to reach their greatest potential for height, vigor and overall appearance in the home landscape, they demand some care—especially when they are young. The difference between a tree that has been well nurtured in its youth and one left to fend for itself can be very apparent. A little care from you at the start will pay off in the long-term health of the tree.

For the first few years of a tree's life, care means fertilizing in spring, summer and fall; generous watering once a week, unless you have a lot of rain; and preventive spraying against disease and insects. On the pages that follow you will find what kind of nutrients trees need and how to apply them; how to mulch so that you conserve moisture, suffocate weeds and stabilize soil temperature, and how to make your own mulch by recycling spent leaves; how to water efficiently; and how to avert the ravages of pests.

Once a tree has established itself, it will be able to stand on its own. It will need watering only in times of drought and spraying only when under attack from pests. Although fertilizing won't hurt, the tree can get by without it because it will be able to store nutrients it draws from the soil, and it will be contributing to the makings of mulch with its falling leaves.

HELPING A TREE TO STRAIGHTEN UP

Three stakes surround a young maple tree and —by means of three wires run through strips of tubing—help it stand straight while it recovers from an injury that gashed its trunk lengthwise.

When you set a young tree in your garden, you may find that the tree bends or even falls over because its trunk is too weak to enable it to stand upright without support. The weakness may be due to crowded growing conditions in the nursery from which you bought it; forced to compete for sunlight, trees stretch upward and become spindly as a result. Or it may be due to injury suffered en route from the nursery to your garden. In either case, staking will correct the problem by helping to brace the trunk and anchor the roots until the tree gains strength.

At first thought it might seem as if staking would be beneficial for any young tree, but this is not the case. Research has shown that trees grow thicker trunks and stronger roots when allowed to bend naturally with the wind. If a tree seems sturdy, leave it unstaked. Then if a strong wind should cause it to lean, you can add stakes to straighten it.

When a tree does need staking, use three stakes rather than just one or two. Use 2-by-2-inch stakes of treated wood or three iron fence posts. In order not to damage the roots, drive the stakes into the ground just outside the root ball; allow about 1 foot in radius for every 1 inch of the trunk's diameter. The wires that will hold the tree should be threaded through a section of rubber tubing to protect the tree bark from damage.

Stakes should be removed just as soon as the tree can hold itself upright. Check deciduous trees after the leaves have dropped in autumn. Untie the wires. If after a few days the tree seems to be listing in one direction or another, retie it to the stakes and check again in the spring. Evergreens can be badly damaged by winter storms. Wait until spring to check them and then, if they have grown strong, remove the stakes permanently.

1 Slide your hand up the trunk of the listing tree *(above, left)*; the place where your hand makes the tree stand straight *(above, right)* is the point where the support tie should be placed. Measure the distance between your hand and the ground and add 24 inches; that will be the length of the stakes you will need.

2 Place three 2-by-2-inch stakes so that they form a triangle just outside the root ball (at least 12 inches from the trunk). Use a mallet to drive each stake into the ground to a depth of 18 inches.

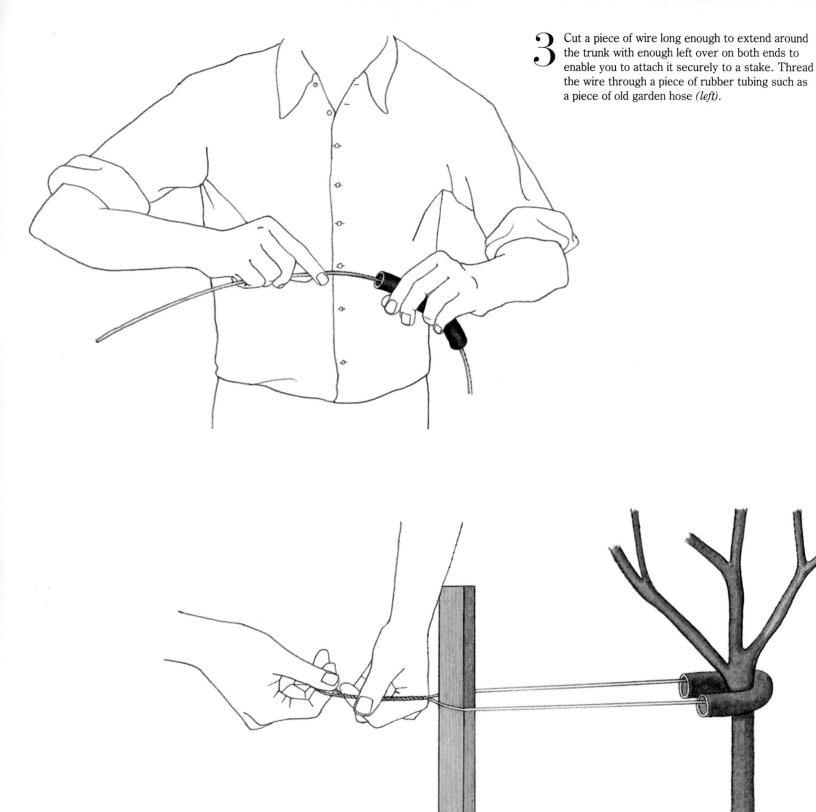

3 Cut a piece of wire long enough to extend around the trunk with enough left over on both ends to enable you to attach it securely to a stake. Thread the wire through a piece of rubber tubing such as a piece of old garden hose *(left)*.

4 Position the rubber tubing so that it covers the middle section of wire—the part of the wire that will go around the tree. Loop the tubing around the trunk, making sure that it protects the trunk from the wire. Adjust the wire so that both ends are of about equal length. Bring the ends of the wire around a stake and twist them together to form a belt enclosing both tree and stake. Fold down the twist against the side of the stake so that you don't have a sharp point protruding. Cut pieces of wire for the other two stakes and repeat the same procedure.

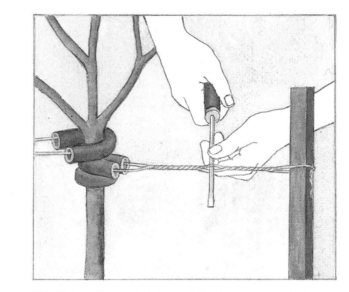

5 If there is any slack in the belts, insert a screwdriver into the space between the strips of wire forming one belt and rotate the screwdriver *(inset);* this will twist the wire and shorten it so that it becomes taut. □

AN ALTERNATIVE METHOD

Another way of staking a tree is to use longer wires and shorter stakes. This method is very good for tall trees. But because wire is less noticeable than stakes, it should be used with caution—and not at all where children play. First, set three 2-by-2-by-18-inch stakes at an angle, 2 to 4 feet away from the trunk, and drive them 12 inches into the ground. Measure the distance from the crotch of the tree to one stake. Double that figure and add an extra 12 inches to allow for twisting. Cut three lengths of wire equal to the resulting figure and thread each one through a piece of rubber tubing. Loop a piece of tubing around a branch at the base of the crotch; lay the other two around the same branch. Secure each wire to its stake and twist the wire to make it taut. For safety's sake you may want to call attention to the wires with red flags.

A NATURAL MULCH
FROM FALLEN LEAVES

A garden that has deciduous trees among its plantings is sure to produce a yardful of leaves each fall. To throw the leaves away is a waste of effort and of good organic material. For no more work than it takes to bag and dispose of them, you can turn the leaves into a soil-improving, tree-nurturing mulch. Several inches of such a mulch spread under a tree can simulate the conditions found on the floor of a thriving forest.

Mulching is good for all trees, but especially for young ones. It insulates the soil against extremes of temperature; it also smothers weeds before they come up. As earthworms and other small creatures break down the organic material, nutrients are added to the soil. At the same time, the products of decomposition improve the soil texture, opening the soil up to air and moisture, promoting good drainage and retarding evaporation.

Raked into a pile and left on their own, leaves will decompose and be ready for use as mulch next season. If you have a shredder, you can hasten the process of decomposition by running the leaves through it and using them right away.

The largest shredders are gasoline-powered and have metal blades that will chip bark and small branches. For leaves alone, a lightweight electric-powered shredder with nylon filament to do the cutting is ideal. It is quieter and easier to use.

Make certain that you have an electrical outlet convenient to your garden; if you need an extension cord, purchase one that is safety-rated for outdoor use. Always wear gloves, goggles and noise guards on your ears to protect your hearing.

A ring of shredded leaf mulch improves the growth prospects for this young dogwood—first, by helping to retain moisture in the soil beneath the tree, and ultimately by enriching the soil as it breaks down.

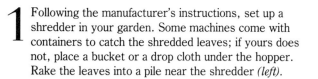

1 Following the manufacturer's instructions, set up a shredder in your garden. Some machines come with containers to catch the shredded leaves; if yours does not, place a bucket or a drop cloth under the hopper. Rake the leaves into a pile near the shredder *(left)*.

2 Be sure you are wearing gloves, goggles and noise guards on your ears. Turn on the shredder and begin feeding leaves into the top, a handful at a time *(above)*. After passing through the shredding element, leaves will drop into the container (or onto the drop cloth) below.

3 Spread a ring of shredded leaves—1 to 2 feet wide and 3 to 4 inches deep—under a young tree *(left)*. Leave a 6-inch-wide strip of uncovered ground directly around the trunk; field mice and other small rodents hide under the mulch, and will gnaw at the bark if they find the trunk too conveniently close. As the mulch decomposes or disperses with the wind, replenish it from time to time. □

FEEDING FOR STRONG ROOTS AND VIGOROUS GROWTH

Supplementing the diet of young trees does wonders for their development. When fertilized three times a year, they shoot up fast—as much as 5 to 6 feet in one season. Fertilizer also benefits mature trees; a dose applied every two or three years will maintain all-round vigor.

All trees take in nutrients through their roots, most of which extend laterally from the trunk to beyond the drip line—the point that lies just beneath the outermost edges of the branches.

The three most important nutrients are nitrogen (for healthy leaves), phosphorus (for healthy roots and blossoms) and potassium (for overall strength and resistance to cold and disease). Fertilizers labeled "complete" contain all three nutrients in any of several ratios. The label "5-10-10" on a bag means it contains 5 percent nitrogen, 10 percent phosphorus and 10 percent potassium. The remaining 75 percent is mostly inert filler—to aid in application—plus trace amounts of other nutrients.

Fertilizer comes in three forms—liquid, which can be sprayed on; solid, which may be slow-release pellets or spikes, which are placed underground; and granulated, which is broadcast by hand. Of the three forms, granulated is the simplest to use. No special equipment is required. You merely sprinkle the granules evenly on the ground above the tree's roots. Keep away from the trunk; fertilizer can burn tender young bark. Water the area immediately so that the fertilizer will soak into the soil.

Young trees should be fertilized once in the spring just before new growth starts, once just after the tree has blossomed and once in the fall just after the leaves start to drop. In all seasons, wait until the ground cover is dry before broadcasting; fertilizer will burn wet grass and the leaves of any living plant on contact.

The large, abundant and leathery leaves of a variegated Norway maple indicate a tree that has been fertilized with a sufficient diet of nitrogen.

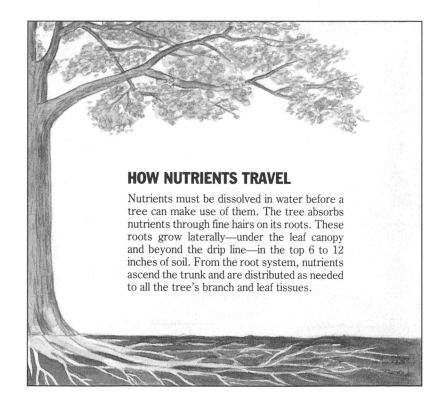

HOW NUTRIENTS TRAVEL

Nutrients must be dissolved in water before a tree can make use of them. The tree absorbs nutrients through fine hairs on its roots. These roots grow laterally—under the leaf canopy and beyond the drip line—in the top 6 to 12 inches of soil. From the root system, nutrients ascend the trunk and are distributed as needed to all the tree's branch and leaf tissues.

ONE WAY TO FERTILIZE

Sprinkle fertilizer in a ring about 6 inches from the tree trunk—keeping the fertilizer a safe distance from the trunk to avoid damaging the bark. A foot or two beyond the drip line, sprinkle a second ring of fertilizer. Fill the area between the two rings with fertilizer, distributing it evenly, a handful at a time. Water immediately. ☐

DRIP LINE

WATERING
DOWN TO THE ROOTS

A young dogwood reaps the benefits of watering that is carefully controlled by means of a single coil of black plastic soaker hose, which lets water seep slowly into the ground at the perimeter of the root system.

Trees stand tall because their roots anchor them firmly in the ground and provide the nutrients they need to live on. But tree roots can only absorb nutrients that are dissolved in water. For the establishment and maintenance of a healthy root system, a ready supply of water is therefore a must.

Young trees need watering frequently; older trees need it only during droughts because their roots reach down deep, where the soil is generally moist. As a rule, a newly transplanted young tree should have water for four hours a day once a week for two or three years, or until it is established. But in sandy soil (which drains quickly) trees need watering more often than in clayey soil (which holds water longer). And the needs of specific trees vary, too. It pays to learn the early symptoms of water deprivation, so that you can take remedial action as soon as possible.

One way to tell if a tree is getting enough water is to check its leaves. Healthy leaves look shiny and feel firm and resilient because of fluid pressure in their green tissues. Lacking enough water to maintain this pressure, the leaves on the very top of the tree and at the ends of branches begin to droop.

For an even earlier sign of water deprivation, test a soil sample from beneath the leaf canopy. With a trowel or a soil auger, dig down about 12 inches; this is where the tree's roots take in water. Squeeze a handful of soil into a ball; open your hand. The soil should hold together in your palm; if it falls apart, it is too dry.

Frequent light waterings (as with a lawn sprinkler) may actually harm trees by encouraging roots to grow too near the surface. For best results, give your tree a long, slow soaking with a soaker hose—one that is made of canvas, or of plastic or rubber that has perforated walls that allow water to seep through. But don't overwater; overwatering can wash vital nutrients from the soil.

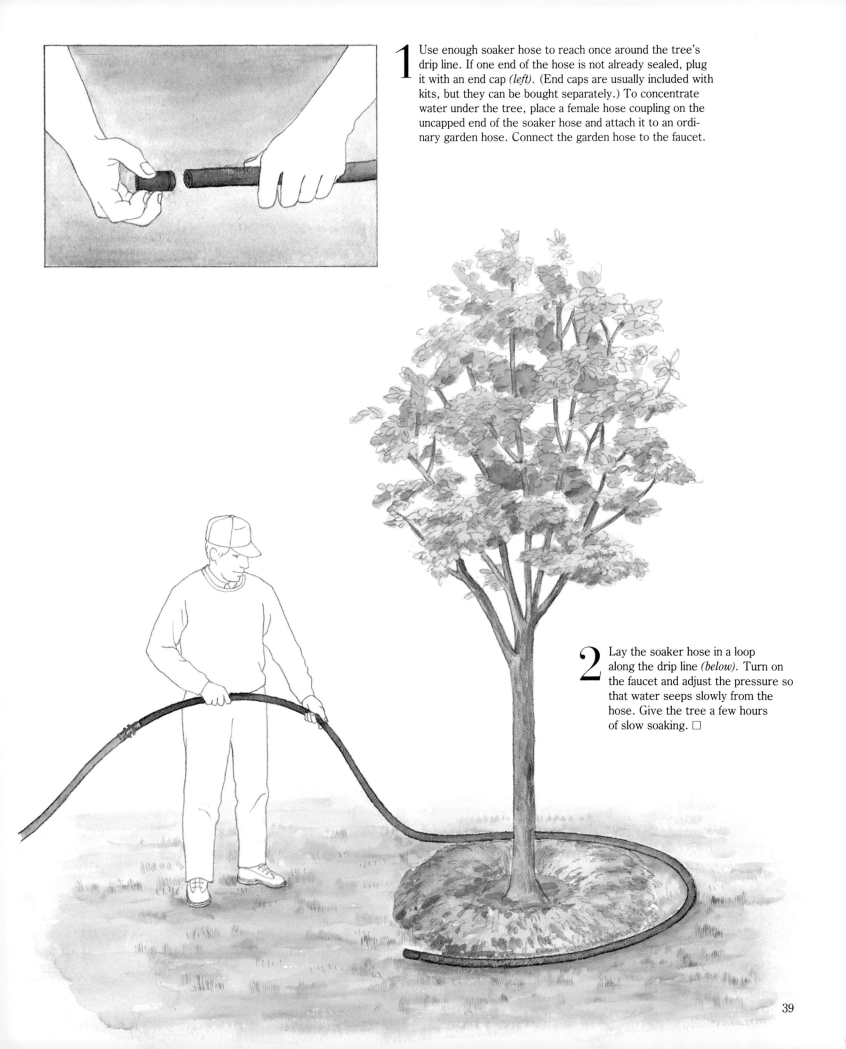

1 Use enough soaker hose to reach once around the tree's drip line. If one end of the hose is not already sealed, plug it with an end cap *(left)*. (End caps are usually included with kits, but they can be bought separately.) To concentrate water under the tree, place a female hose coupling on the uncapped end of the soaker hose and attach it to an ordinary garden hose. Connect the garden hose to the faucet.

2 Lay the soaker hose in a loop along the drip line *(below)*. Turn on the faucet and adjust the pressure so that water seeps slowly from the hose. Give the tree a few hours of slow soaking. □

GETTING RID OF GARDEN PESTS

Spring and summer are the best of times for home gardeners. But the seasons of growth and ripening are also prime seasons for insect infestations. Some insects attack foliage, others flowers, others bark. With the right insecticide, you can fight back against the pests that threaten your plants and trees. But take care when choosing and using these powerful weapons; you want to make sure it's only the pests that get hurt.

There are many kinds of insecticides on the market, and not all are safe for home use. Read the label of any bottle of insecticide carefully before buying it. Avoid synthetic insecticides. These are based on chemicals—chlorinated hydrocarbons, organophosphates and carbamates—that can harm people, wildlife and beneficial insects.

Look for insecticides that are derived from natural sources and that are nontoxic except to the targeted pests. Some of these contain hormones that disrupt an invading pest's reproductive cycle; others rely on microorganisms that cause insect diseases or substances made by plants that have evolved natural defenses against insect enemies— like the pyrethrins extracted from chrysanthemums.

The safest of all insecticides for home use is one called horticultural oil, which is available at garden centers. A layer of this oil suffocates a variety of pests, especially scale insects that attack bark and twigs. Apply it on a windless day with a 1- to 1½-gallon compression sprayer.

Even with nontoxic insecticides, be sure to follow label instructions for recommended uses, times and methods of application, and precautions.

The lush blossoms and thick bark on this Japanese flowering cherry indicate a healthy tree (the horizontal striations on the bark are characteristic of the species). Scale insects sometimes invade tree bark in winter and can destroy the whole tree, but spraying with horticultural oil will smother them and any eggs they lay.

1 Before spraying horticultural oil, don a face mask and goggles to prevent oil particles from getting into your lungs and eyes. For added protection, wear long pants, a long-sleeved shirt and rubber gloves. Unscrew the top of a compression sprayer. Measure oil according to instructions on the insecticide bottle and pour it into the sprayer *(left)*. Fill the sprayer with water from a garden hose.

2 Replace the top of the compression sprayer and screw it on tightly. Holding onto the container with one hand, pump the handle several times with the other hand until you cannot pump any more.

3 Spray an even coat of oil mixture over the bark of the tree. After spraying, unscrew the container top and dispose of any leftover mixture as recommended on the insecticide label. Rinse the container thoroughly and hang it upside down to drain. Store it when it is dry. □

3
PRUNING TREES

P runing is the art of gently guiding a tree into its best possible shape, not by drastically altering its natural growth habit, but by skillfully modifying and making the most of it. Too often, though, pruning turns into a confrontation between gardener and plant, and the plant comes out the worse for wear. The difference between frustrating struggle and rewarding craft is a little specialized knowledge. Learning just a few simple techniques will give you the skill to tackle any pruning job.

How you cut affects the growth of a tree, and certain types of trees require special kinds of pruning. Because their new growth comes from the tips of their branches, evergreens need to be treated in a different manner from deciduous trees. Younger trees are usually pruned to guide their strength; in older trees, the need for pruning is often the result of disease or damage. On the following pages are directions for handling both.

To do the job right you'll need a good set of sharp tools: a pair of pruning shears for small branches and twigs and a curved-blade pruning saw for larger branches. There are also special long-handled shears and pole saws that will extend your reach to high branches. With all tools, make sure the blades are clean and sharp; dirty and dull edges can damage your trees and give insects and disease an easy entry.

TRIMMING
UNWANTED STEMS

This weeping cherry tree owes its clean trunk and elegant outline to conscientious pruning of suckers that would otherwise deplete the tree's energy.

Suckers are thin stems that grow up toward the light from a tree's roots or from the base of its trunk. Besides being unsightly, suckers (as their name implies) draw energy from roots and crown and thus can weaken a tree. Removing them ensures that the tree will develop from one large trunk, which gives a much neater appearance. Fruit trees are especially prone to suckers. That is because fruit trees are often propagated by grafting trees having different characteristics *(pages 74-81)*. The suckers of a grafted tree will resemble the character of the rootstock—the tree likely to have been chosen more for hardiness than for appearance—and if left alone will drive out the characteristics intended in the grafting. You will want to remove the suckers immediately.

Fortunately, pruning suckers is easy if you have the right tools. For the thinnest stems (no more than 1 inch in diameter) use a pair of pruning shears; for larger suckers, you will need a curved pruning saw. Look for well-made tools with high-quality steel blades. Good tools make clean cuts, which heal faster than ragged cuts, and therefore reduce the risk of disease.

Horticulturists nowadays generally advise against an old-fashioned practice of painting over pruning cuts; modern experiments have shown that so-called wound dressings actually interfere with the tree's natural healing process.

No matter how thorough you are, you can expect suckers to grow back. When they do, prune them again.

1 With a pair of pruning shears, snip off a thin sucker as low on its stem as possible *(left)*. You can even brush away some soil to ensure that you are removing the full length of the sucker. To make the smallest, cleanest cut, snip straight across rather than at an angle.

2 For suckers more than 1 inch in diameter, use a curved-blade pruning saw *(right)*. Make the cut as close to the trunk as possible. Be prepared to repeat the job whenever the suckers grow back —as they almost always do. □

TOOLS FOR PRUNING

PRUNING SHEARS

For removing slender suckers. The best shears have stainless-steel blades. Most are 7 to 9 inches long including handles, and fit nicely in your back pocket. Be sure the shears are closed and locked before pocketing them.

CURVED SAW

For removing thick suckers. The best saws have flexible blades of tempered steel, with six teeth to the inch. The teeth usually have beveled cutting edges and are angled so that they do all the work on the pull, not the push.

FOLDING SAW

Works like a standard curved-blade pruning saw and is made of the same materials: tempered steel for the blade, ash or hickory for the handle. When the blade is folded and secured, the saw can be safely carried in a pants or jacket pocket.

SHAPING
A NEEDLE-LEAVED EVERGREEN

Some judicious pruning, especially in the early years, will help the health of almost any tree and encourage it into a compact yet natural-looking silhouette. The techniques of pruning, however, differ with different kinds of trees.

Deciduous trees and broad-leaved evergreens put out buds all along their branches. Cutting just beyond a bud will promote new growth in a predictable direction; it will encourage the remaining buds to bloom and the branch to put out more buds.

In general, needle-leaved evergreens need less training than their broad-leaved cousins to keep them in shape. Those that are fine-needled and send shoots out in all directions along their branches—such as hemlocks, yews and arborvitae—need only be sheared at the tips from time to time. But certain others—pines, spruce and firs—put out new growth only at the ends of their limbs. Every spring each branch tip produces a new growth called a candle— a cylindrical shoot that develops into a branch during the summer.

Pruning pines, spruce, firs and similar needle-leaved evergreens involves selective and careful cutting of the candles. When done correctly it can help control a tree's size and shape. If you cut off part of a candle, the remainder hardens and becomes a branch; and that branch will produce a new candle the following spring. But if you cut off a branch beyond a candle it cannot produce a new one.

Pruning is most effective when started early in the life of a tree. Damaged and unshapely branches can be pruned any time of the year *(right)*. Pruning for shape *(opposite)* should be done in spring.

Upright candles on this Austrian pine are ready for pinching off. Similar pruning in previous springs has resulted in the close, dense growth seen here.

WHERE TO PRUNE

A branch pruned from a needle-leaved evergreen will never grow beyond the cut. Candidates for pruning include weather-damaged branches, branches that stray from a desired silhouette *(right)* and branches that obstruct a pathway. Cut 1 inch above a fork formed by two lateral branches *(above)*. For branches thicker than 1 inch in diameter, use a pruning saw.

1 To train a young pine to assume a compact shape as it matures, prune its candles (new growth shoots) every spring *(right)*. Wait until the candles reach a length of about 4 inches; then break them in half *(above)*.

2 Once a needle-leaved evergreen has grown to within inches of the size you want it to be, you can prevent further growth by breaking off each of its candles close to its base *(left)*. Repeat every spring as soon as new candles appear. The tree will maintain its height, shape and vigorous appearance. □

REMOVING LIMBS
FROM A MATURE TREE

There are a number of reasons for pruning a large limb from a mature tree. The limb may be diseased or damaged; it may be interfering with a view, growing into a roof or a chimney (which makes it a fire hazard), casting unwanted shadows or blocking the breezes that cool a patio. Or the limb may be a hazard to the tree itself. A branch that forms a narrow V-shaped crotch with the trunk instead of a wide-angled L is vulnerable to injury from accumulated ice and snow, and may have to be removed before it breaks off.

For most trees, the best time to do such surgery is when they are dormant, usually winter or early spring. Before cutting off a large branch, examine it carefully. Look for its branch collar—a swelling where the branch attaches to the trunk. Make your cut close to the branch collar but never into it; the collar contains substances that will help the tree seal and heal the wound. Leave the wound open to the sun and air; tree "dressings" only hinder the natural healing process. To keep the wound as small as possible, avoid tearing off surrounding bark. If the branch is a heavy one, remove it in two sections, with a sequence of carefully spaced cuts, as shown here. For limbs up to 10 inches in diameter, use a pruning saw; for ones larger than that, use a bow saw *(box, right)*. Make sure before you begin that the ground is clear; tools can be damaged and human beings injured by the force of a falling limb.

A Babylon weeping willow shows strong limbs and rounded crown—characteristics preserved by periodic pruning of crossing, damaged and weak branches.

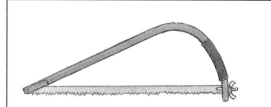

A BOW SAW
FOR THICK LIMBS

For cutting thick limbs—those that are 10 to 25 inches in diameter—a bow saw is ideal. It consists of a curved steel frame, a thin, flexible, toothed blade and a nut that locks the blade in place. The frame gives tension to the blade, and its tapered nose can slip with ease past other branches on the tree.

1 For control, prune a heavy branch in stages. Make a first cut on the underside of the branch, 12 inches from the trunk and ½ to 1 inch deep. Put all your energy into pulling the saw; a pruning saw's teeth cut only on the pull stroke.

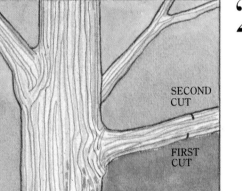

SECOND CUT

FIRST CUT

2 Place your second cut on the upper surface of the branch, about 14 inches away from the trunk (left). Saw downward; as you approach the lower cut, the branch will fall, leaving a temporarily protruding 12- to 14-inch stub.

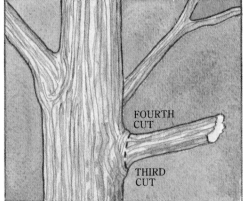

FOURTH CUT

THIRD CUT

3 To finish the job, cut the stub back to the branch collar. Make a cut from underneath, ½ to 1 inch deep; then make a final cut from the top, sawing completely through the branch. If possible, angle the final cut so that it meets the previous cut. □

THINNING BRANCHES FOR LIGHT AND AIR

The ideally shaped tree generally has one main leader (the trunk) and, depending on species and size, a number of major lateral branches extending from it. A somewhat open shape is not only eye-pleasing; it promotes the health of the tree by admitting light to the leaves and branches and improving air circulation. Such a shape can be achieved by selective thinning —that is, removing entire branches at their point of origin.

Thinning should be started when a tree is young and healthy. All dead limbs and any branches that point inward or rub against other branches should be removed. When choosing between two interfering branches, always prune the weaker of the pair. Make a clean cut just outside the branch collar—the swelling where the branch extends from the trunk.

Keep the tree's wounds as small as possible. To avoid stripping bark when cutting a large branch, remove the heaviest branches in sections with a sequence of carefully spaced cuts *(page 49)* and support the branch with one hand while cutting or sawing with the other hand. And for your own safety, wear sturdy gloves, long pants and a long-sleeved shirt.

As a rule, trees should be pruned only during dormant periods. This means before new growth begins in the spring and after leaves have dropped in the autumn. Some exceptions are birches, beeches and maples, which tend to bleed sap when cut. They should be thinned in late spring or early summer; they bleed less when in full leaf.

A mature plum tree reaps the benefits of early thinning, which opens the structure to sun and air and clears the way for such spirited efflorescence.

AVOIDING UNSIGHTLY SPROUTS

Incorrect pruning—ripping branches from the trunk, removing a large upright limb from a horizontal branch, excessive thinning—can lead to unattractive water sprouts. These are thin upright shoots that weaken major lateral branches, deplete a tree's energy and mar its shape. To guard against water sprouts, never prune more than one-third of a tree's branches at any one time. If sprouts appear, remove them immediately with pruning shears.

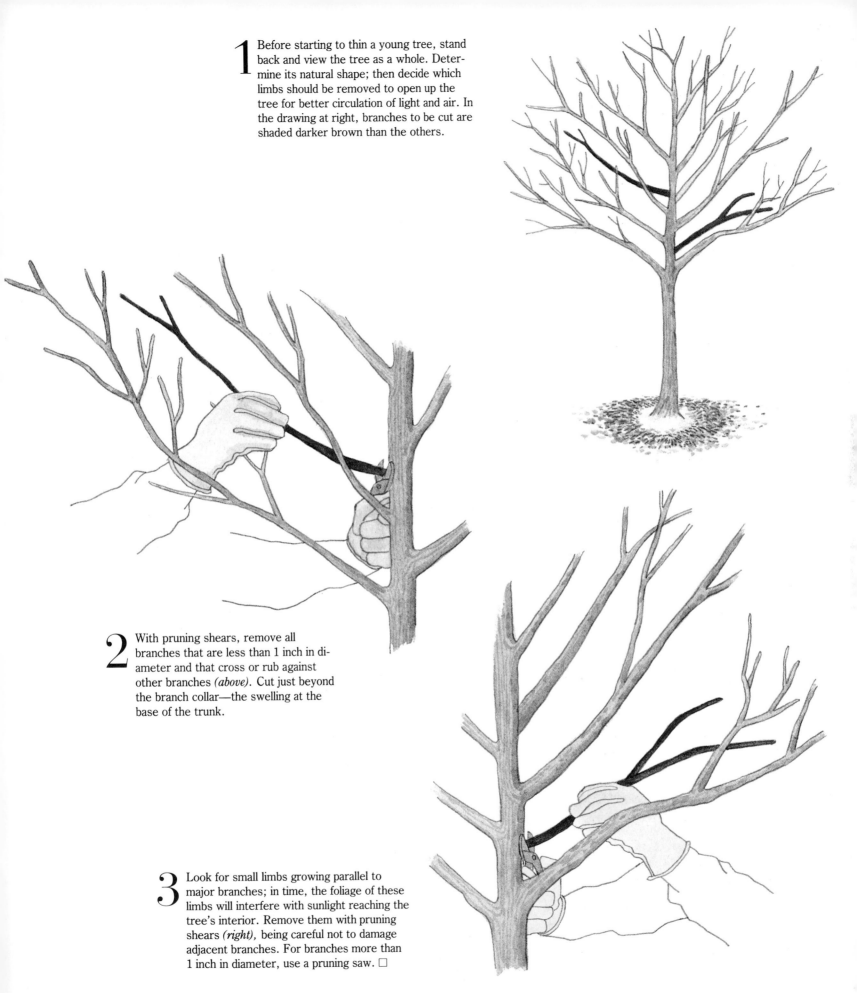

1 Before starting to thin a young tree, stand back and view the tree as a whole. Determine its natural shape; then decide which limbs should be removed to open up the tree for better circulation of light and air. In the drawing at right, branches to be cut are shaded darker brown than the others.

2 With pruning shears, remove all branches that are less than 1 inch in diameter and that cross or rub against other branches *(above)*. Cut just beyond the branch collar—the swelling at the base of the trunk.

3 Look for small limbs growing parallel to major branches; in time, the foliage of these limbs will interfere with sunlight reaching the tree's interior. Remove them with pruning shears *(right)*, being careful not to damage adjacent branches. For branches more than 1 inch in diameter, use a pruning saw. □

51

A STRATEGIC CUT FOR DIRECTING GROWTH

Heading back—cutting off the end of a branch just beyond a bud—is a method of pruning that gives you control of a tree's growth pattern. It is used to modify the shape of deciduous trees and broad-leaved evergreens. (For needle-leaved evergreens, see pages 46-47.)

By placing cuts with care, you can not only encourage vigorous growth but channel that growth to produce a fuller, more compact tree—a profile especially suited for showing off a profusion of spring or summer flowers.

How a branch grows after it has been headed back is determined by the orientation of its terminal bud. Buds grow all around the circumference of a branch. If a vertical branch is cut back to an outward-facing bud, the new growth will be outward. If you want a horizontal branch to grow upward, cut it back to an upward-facing bud.

Most trees may be headed back at any time of the year. Spring-flowering trees such as crabapple, dogwood, cherry and pear are exceptions; they should be pruned just after they finish blooming in spring. Make your cut about ¼ inch above the bud you have selected and at a 45° angle slanting downward so that rainwater will not collect in the wound. To hasten healing, leave the wound exposed to sun and air, without tree paint. Never remove more than one-third of the tree's total growth at one time; if too much is removed, the tree will use its energy to produce water sprouts *(page 50)*.

The limbs of a newly planted tree should be cut to two-thirds of their original length; this lessens the workload on the roots and helps them recover more quickly from transplant shock. But check first with your nursery or garden center; some trees are pruned before being offered for sale and you don't want it done twice.

A European beech displays a symmetrical, natural-looking silhouette—its growth having been tamed by the pruning back of selected limbs.

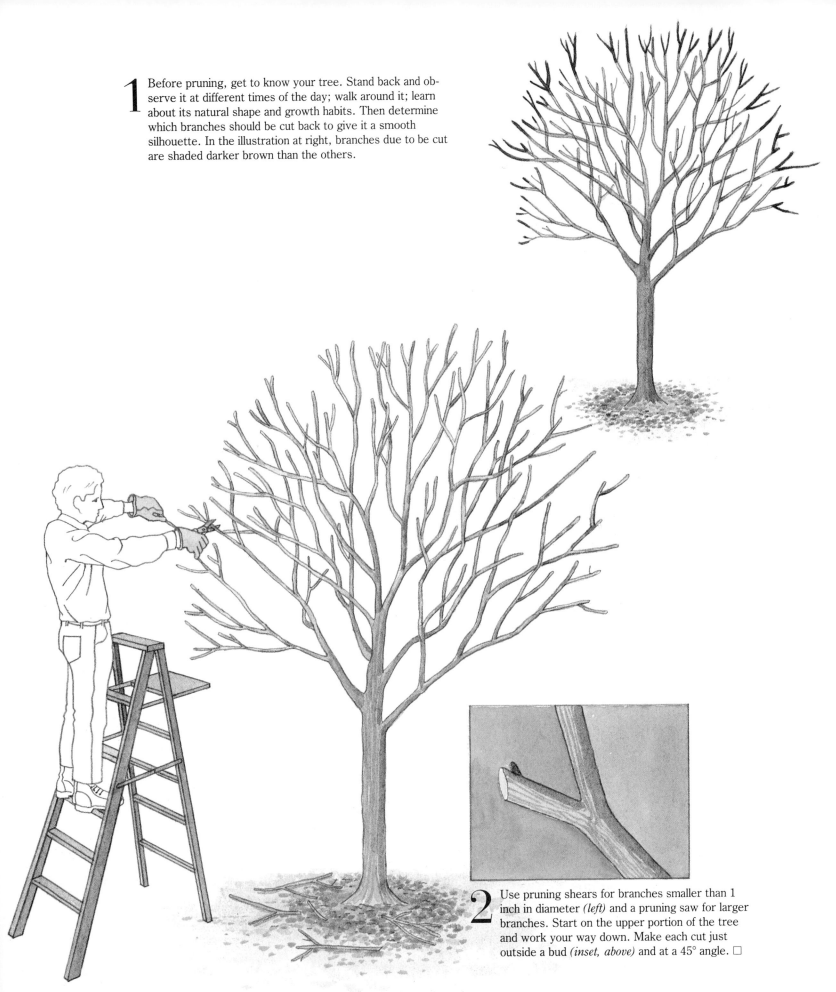

1 Before pruning, get to know your tree. Stand back and observe it at different times of the day; walk around it; learn about its natural shape and growth habits. Then determine which branches should be cut back to give it a smooth silhouette. In the illustration at right, branches due to be cut are shaded darker brown than the others.

2 Use pruning shears for branches smaller than 1 inch in diameter *(left)* and a pruning saw for larger branches. Start on the upper portion of the tree and work your way down. Make each cut just outside a bud *(inset, above)* and at a 45° angle. □

53

4
NEW TREES
FROM OLD

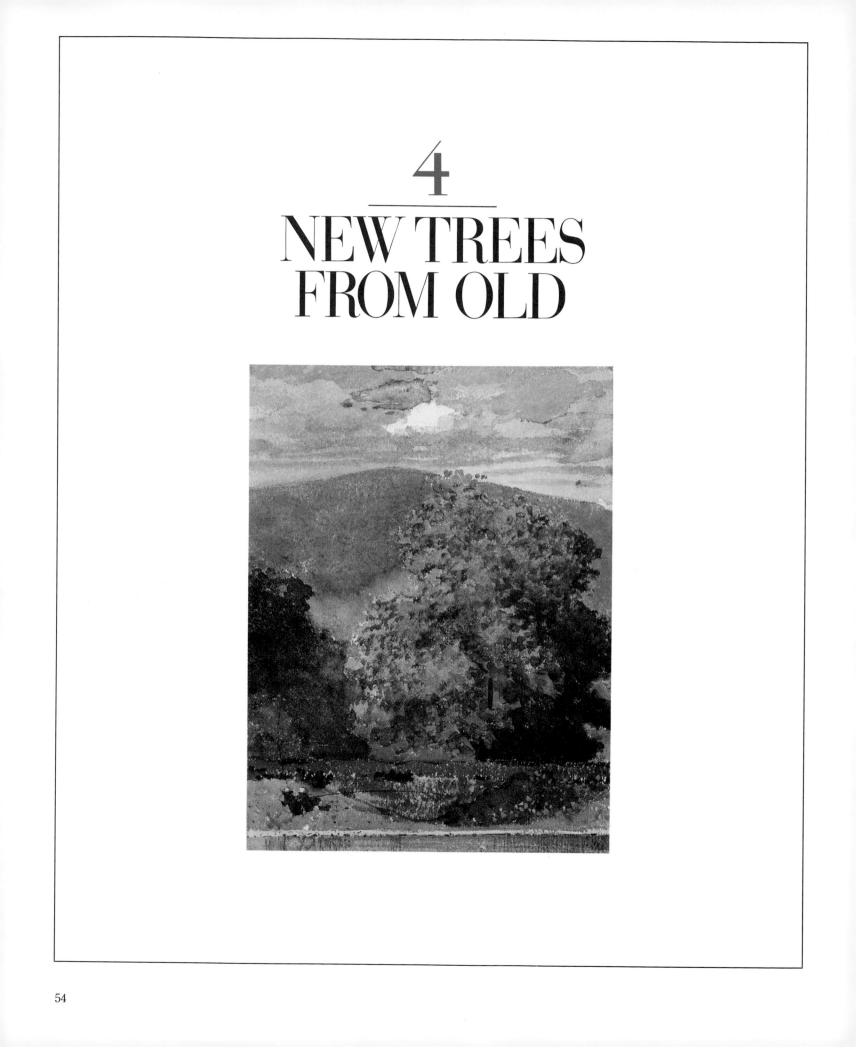

Propagation may seem a mysterious science best left to professional growers. But if you enjoy experimenting, don't mind trial and error, and are patient, you may find that propagating your own plants holds many rewards. Growing a tree from seed or watching a cutting take root can kindle enormous excitement. Doing your own propagation takes considerably more time than driving to the local nursery for a new tree, but the sense of accomplishment when a tree has sprouted makes it worth trying.

Many trees can be grown from seed, and virtually all the trees in your garden drop seeds from time to time. There are several techniques for collecting and for hastening the process of propagation. Once seeds are sprouted and growing, and you have selected the healthiest and most vigorous ones, it is a simple matter to transplant the young seedlings into individual pots, and eventually into the soil.

In addition to growing trees from seed, there are a number of methods that are collectively called vegetative propagation. They include taking stem cuttings, and grafting from scions and from buds. With these vegetative propagation methods, you take a part of the parent tree and clone it into a separate plant. One advantage of vegetative propagation is that you can duplicate a favored tree exactly. Another is that vegetative propagation usually gives you a planting-sized tree faster than one you might grow from a seed of the same tree.

The techniques for practicing these methods are explained on the pages that follow.

COLLECTING SEEDS FOR A START

New trees do not have to come partially grown from mail-order firms or nurseries. Some varieties are easier to begin than others. Almost any tree that bears fruit—including berries and cones—can be grown from seed, if you like to experiment.

Seeds for trees can be purchased from garden supply companies. But it is both less expensive and more exciting to collect seeds from trees in the backyard, in nearby woodlands or even in public parks. And collecting has another benefit: seeds found locally will be from trees acclimated to the region.

The essence of collecting seeds is to get them while they are ripe—but before breezes have blown them about, or birds and squirrels have done their filching. Most wind-dispersed seeds ripen in the autumn and most signal their readiness by turning from green to tan or brown. To collect the seeds in pods or capsules, shake a few branches and collect the fallout on an old sheet or a tarpaulin spread below.

For conifers, pick some cones when they are brown and semidry but before they have opened. Dry them on a raised wire screen (to promote air circulation) placed in the sun or in a warm shed. When the cones pop open, shake the seeds onto a piece of newspaper. Magnolias, which are not strictly speaking conifers, produce large pods that somewhat resemble cones. The pods, like cones, should be collected when they turn red or brown, and before they open and release their seeds. They should then be dried in the same way that cones are dried.

The fleshy fruits or berries produced by other trees should be collected when they turn color—from green to red or some other hue. The seeds must then be removed from the fruit, as shown at right and on the following pages. How various seeds need to be prepared for planting—and the best methods for planting them—are explained on subsequent pages.

Its branches stripped of leaves by autumn winds, an iigiri tree displays a lavish crop of red fruits. The fruits can be macerated to yield seeds that, if carefully chosen and nurtured, can be planted to produce more trees like the parent.

1 To collect seeds from a holly (or any other tree that produces fruitlike pods or berries), pick the berries and examine them to make sure they are healthy. If you are collecting from trees of different species, place the fruits of different trees in separate bags, and label each bag so you will know what you have when you are ready to plant.

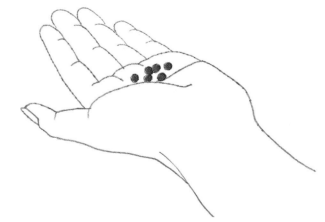

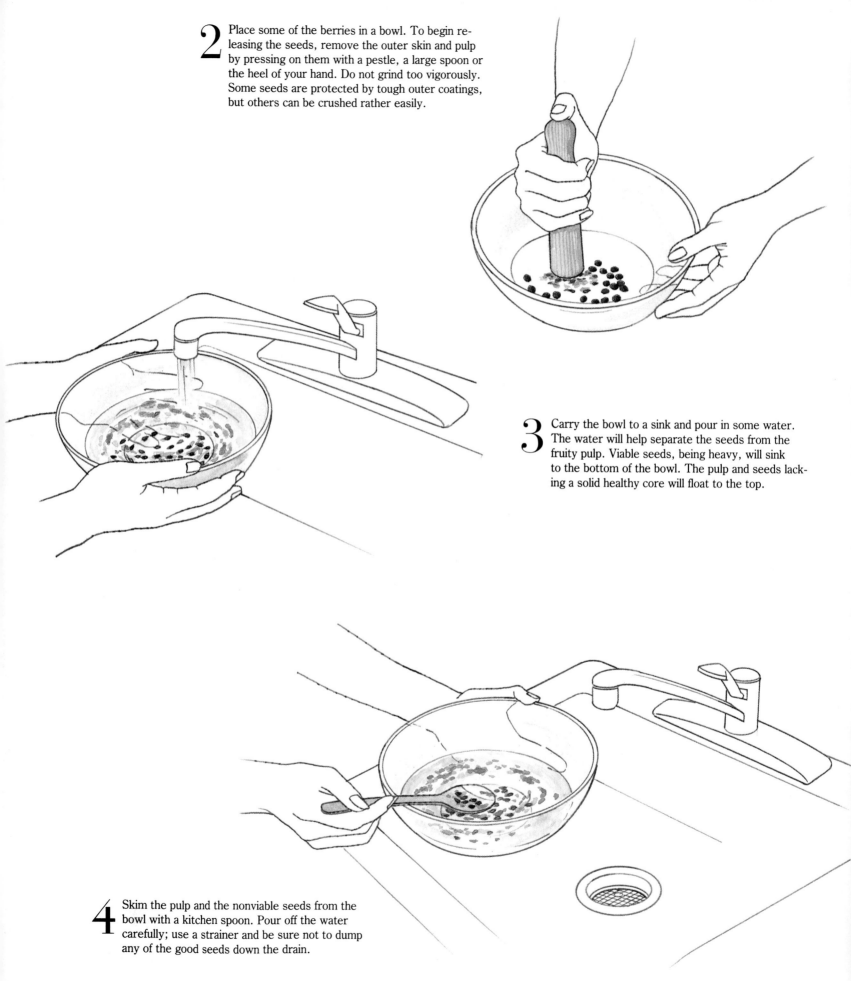

2 Place some of the berries in a bowl. To begin releasing the seeds, remove the outer skin and pulp by pressing on them with a pestle, a large spoon or the heel of your hand. Do not grind too vigorously. Some seeds are protected by tough outer coatings, but others can be crushed rather easily.

3 Carry the bowl to a sink and pour in some water. The water will help separate the seeds from the fruity pulp. Viable seeds, being heavy, will sink to the bottom of the bowl. The pulp and seeds lacking a solid healthy core will float to the top.

4 Skim the pulp and the nonviable seeds from the bowl with a kitchen spoon. Pour off the water carefully; use a strainer and be sure not to dump any of the good seeds down the drain.

5 Remove the viable seeds from the bowl and spread them on a paper towel. Leave them for a few days, until they are thoroughly dry.

6 Place the seeds in airtight containers, sprinkle a fungicide over the seeds, and label and date the containers. Some seeds will remain viable for up to two years and can be stored in the refrigerator. Some need special treatment called stratification and scarification *(pages 60-63)*. Others must be planted right away *(box, below)*. □

FOR PLANTING RIGHT AWAY

Seeds of almost 20 kinds of trees do not store well at all. Seeds from these trees, which are listed below, should be planted immediately on being collected.

American beech	Japanese zelkova
Atlas cedar	Lacebark pine
Bur oak	Lodgepole pine
Cedar of Lebanon	Red buckeye
Chinese chestnut	River birch
Chinese evergreen oak	Sawtooth oak
European beech	Southern live oak
European hornbeam	White oak
Franklin tree	Willow
Japanese maple	

BRINGING DORMANT SEEDS TO LIFE

Some tree seeds are ready to germinate soon after they fall from their branches and should be planted immediately *(box, page 59)*. But a majority need time for their embryos to ripen. Fortunately there are ways to hurry these slow-maturing seeds so that the ones you collect in the summer or fall will be ready to plant the following spring.

One method of hastening germination is known as scarification, in which you score the seed *(box, opposite)*. Another is known as cold stratification, in which you simulate the conditions of winter, as shown in the steps opposite. Certain seeds must be cool and moist for a period of time before they can germinate. In nature, they stay cool and wet in winter under layers of leaves and snow. Cold stratification involves placing seeds in plastic bags with some damp sphagnum moss *(opposite)* and keeping them at 34° to 40° F—the temperature range inside most refrigerators.

The seeds of various trees require different lengths of this wintry treatment. For example, spruce, golden larch and cypress seeds need to be kept cool for three weeks to two months; fir, hickory and hornbeam for between one and three months; walnut, smoke tree, horse chestnut, soapberry and mountain ash for three to four months.

The seeds of some other trees undergo a process called double dormancy. The embryos go through one phase struggling to produce root structures and then another producing shoots. For them, logically enough, a double germinating process is needed. First, the bagged seeds should be stored in a warm environment (65° to 85° F) for two or more months, then in a refrigerator for an additional length of time. Timing is important. The process should be started just long enough before spring planting to give the seeds the proper interval to germinate and become ready to grow. To be sure how long any given seed needs to go through this hot-cold treatment, consult the chart on pages 62-63.

A small Japanese maple casts shade on a grassy lawn in summer, and drops its seeds in autumn. The seeds, if stored at controlled temperatures (a treatment called stratification), will germinate and produce new trees.

CRACKING TOUGH CASES

Whether they must be planted immediately or need cold stratification, any tree seeds encased in coverings so hard that you cannot pierce them with your thumbnail will need to be scarified— that is, scarred, or cracked—before they will germinate. To scarify, rub the hard coating against a file or the edge of a piece of folded sandpaper until small breaks appear. The breaks will allow moisture and oxygen to penetrate, spurring seed growth. Before putting the seeds in the ground, soak them in water for 15 minutes.

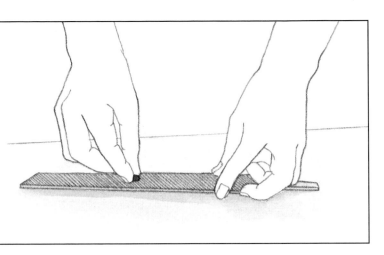

1 Moisten some sphagnum moss by dipping it, a handful at a time, in a bucket of water. Squeeze out the excess water while still leaving the moss wet and spongy.

2 Place the moss in plastic bags, then mix in your seeds, one species per bag. Close the bags so that they are airtight. Label them, including the date and the period required for the seeds to germinate. Put the bags away—in the refrigerator if they are seeds that need a cool environment, on a shelf somewhere in the house if they need a warm one. □

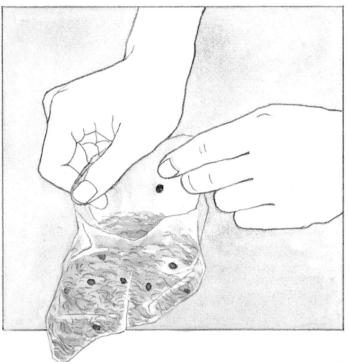

A GUIDE TO TREATING DORMANT SEEDS

To sprout, some seeds require a period of stratification—that is, embedding in one or more layers of moist sphagnum moss or other organic matter while they emerge from dormancy. All such seeds need a period of cold stratification; some need a prior period of warm stratification. The approximate times for both are given below. From warm stratification seeds will be ready to move to cold when they have sprouted roots. From cold stratification seeds will be ready to plant when they have sprouted both roots and stems.

TREE	SEED TREATMENT
ABIES Fir	One to three months of cold stratification.
ACACIA Acacia, wattle	Two to four months of cold stratification.
ACER Maple	Three months of warm stratification followed by three to six months of cold stratification, except for red maple and silver maple, which do not need stratifying.
AESCULUS Horse chestnut, buckeye	Four months of cold stratification, except for red buckeye, which does not need stratifying.
AILANTHUS Tree-of-heaven	Two months of cold stratification.
ALNUS Alder	Two to three months of cold stratification.
AMELANCHIER Serviceberry, Juneberry, shadbush	Two to six months of cold stratification.
ARALIA	Three months of cold stratification.
ARBUTUS Manzanita	Three months of cold stratification.
CARPINUS Hornbeam	One to two months of warm stratification followed by two to four months of cold stratification.
CARYA Hickory	One to three months of cold stratification.
CASTANEA Chestnut	Two to three months of cold stratification.
CELTIS Hackberry	Three months of cold stratification.
CERCIS Redbud	Two to three months of cold stratification.
CHAMAECYPARIS False cypress	One month of warm stratification followed by one month of cold stratification except for Lawson false cypress and sawara false cypress, which do not need stratifying.
CORNUS Dogwood	Two months of warm stratification followed by two to four months of cold stratification.

TREE	SEED TREATMENT
CORYLUS Filbert, hazelnut	Two to six months of cold stratification.
COTINUS Smoke tree	Three months of cold stratification.
CRATAEGUS Hawthorn	Three to six months of cold stratification.
CRYPTOMERIA	Three months of warm stratification followed by three months of cold stratification.
CUNNINGHAMIA China fir	One month of cold stratification.
CUPRESSUS Cypress	Three weeks of cold stratification.
DAVIDIA	Five months of warm stratification followed by three months of cold stratification.
DIOSPYROS Persimmon	Two to three months of cold stratification required only for common persimmon.
ELAEAGNUS	Two to three months of cold stratification.
FRANKLINIA	One month of cold stratification.
FRAXINUS Ash	One to three months of warm stratification followed by two to three months of cold stratification, except for flowering ash and green ash, which require two to three months of cold stratification. No stratifying is required for shamel ash.
GINKGO Ginkgo, maidenhair tree	One to two months of warm stratification followed by one to two months of cold stratification.
HALESIA Silverbell, snowdrop tree	Two to four months of warm stratification followed by four to five months of cold stratification.
ILEX Holly	Two months of warm stratification followed by two months of cold stratification.
JUGLANS Walnut	Three to four months of cold stratification.
JUNIPERUS Juniper	One to four months of cold stratification.

TREE	SEED TREATMENT
LAGERSTROEMIA Crape myrtle	One month of cold stratification.
LARIX Larch	One to two months of cold stratification.
LIQUIDAMBAR Sweet gum	One to three months of cold stratification.
LIRIODENDRON Tulip tree	Two to three months of cold stratification.
MAGNOLIA	Three to six months of cold stratification.
MALUS Flowering crabapple	One to four months of cold stratification.
METASEQUOIA Dawn redwood	One month of cold stratification.
MORUS Mulberry	One to three month of cold stratification.
NYSSA Tupelo	One month of cold stratification.
OSTRYA Hop hornbeam	Three months of warm stratification followed by three to five months of cold stratification.
PARROTIA	Five months of warm stratification followed by three months of cold stratification.
PHELLODENDRON Cork tree	Two months of cold stratification.
PICEA Spruce	Three weeks of cold stratification.
PINUS Pine	One-half to three months of cold stratification, except for Swiss stone pine, which may need up to nine months, and for Japanese red pine, lacebark pine and lodgepole pine, which do not need stratifying.
PISTACIA Pistache	Two months of cold stratification.
PLATANUS Sycamore, button-wood, plane tree	Two to three months of cold stratification.
PRUNUS	Three to six months of cold stratification, except for Amur chokeberry, which requires four months of warm stratification followed by three months of cold stratification.
PSEUDOLARIX Golden larch	One to two months of cold stratification.

TREE	SEED TREATMENT
PSEUDOTSUGA	Two months of cold stratification.
PTEROSTYRAX Epaulette tree	Three months of cold stratification.
PYRUS Pear	One month of cold stratification.
QUERCUS Oak	One to six months of cold stratification.
SABAL Palmetto	One month of cold stratification.
SAPINDUS Soapberry	Three months of cold stratification.
SAPIUM	One month of cold stratification.
SASSAFRAS	Four months of cold stratification.
SCIADOPITYS	Three months of cold stratification.
SORBUS Mountain ash	Three months of cold stratification.
STEWARTIA	Four months of warm stratification followed by three months of cold stratification.
STYRAX Snowbell	Three to five months of warm stratification followed by three months of cold stratification.
SYRINGA Lilac	One to three months of cold stratification.
TAXODIUM Cypress	Three months of cold stratification.
TAXUS Yew	Four months of warm stratification followed by four months of cold stratification.
THUJA Arborvitae	One to two months of cold stratification.
TSUGA Hemlock	One to four months of cold stratification.
ULMUS Elm	Two to three months of cold stratification required only for American elm.
VIBURNUM	Five to nine months of warm stratification followed by one to two months of cold stratification.
WASHINGTONIA Washington fan palm	Three months of cold stratification.
ZELKOVA	Two months of cold stratification.

IMPROVING THE ODDS BY STARTING SEEDS INDOORS

Growing trees from seeds has some of the excitement and allure of a lottery. How many will sprout, and how healthy will the seedlings be? One thing is certain: not all of them will come up. In the wild, only a very few of the thousands of seeds a tree scatters each year ever manage to produce another tree.

The odds are vastly improved, though, if the seeds have been carefully collected and nurtured—as shown in the previous sections of this chapter. Especially important is well-timed stratification *(pages 60-63).* Seeds properly coaxed through dormancy should be ready to germinate when planting time arrives in the spring.

The odds for success are even better when seeds are started in containers indoors, safely beyond the reach of the birds, rodents, wintry winds and early-spring downpours that kill many outdoor seedlings. Any of several kinds of containers can be used—clay pots, plastic pots, shallow trays, cutoff milk cartons—so long as they have holes in the bottom. If you use a container that has been used before, it should be given a thorough washing and a rinse with one part chlorine bleach to 10 parts water to kill any lingering pests.

The best potting medium is the sort of premoistened soilless mixture of peat moss and vermiculite sold at garden centers. It is disease-free, and light and loose enough to let the seeds sprout easily.

Depending on the species, the seeds may sprout in a week or after several months. In planting *(opposite),* you can increase the odds of success once more by putting in extra seeds, say three or four to a pot instead of one. Some may not sprout at all; others may produce weak seedlings. Simply select the best ones when transplanting time comes, as explained on pages 66-69.

A number of six-week-old Canada hemlock seedlings thrust their way through a light planting medium in a terra-cotta pot. As the needles develop, the seedpods will drop off.

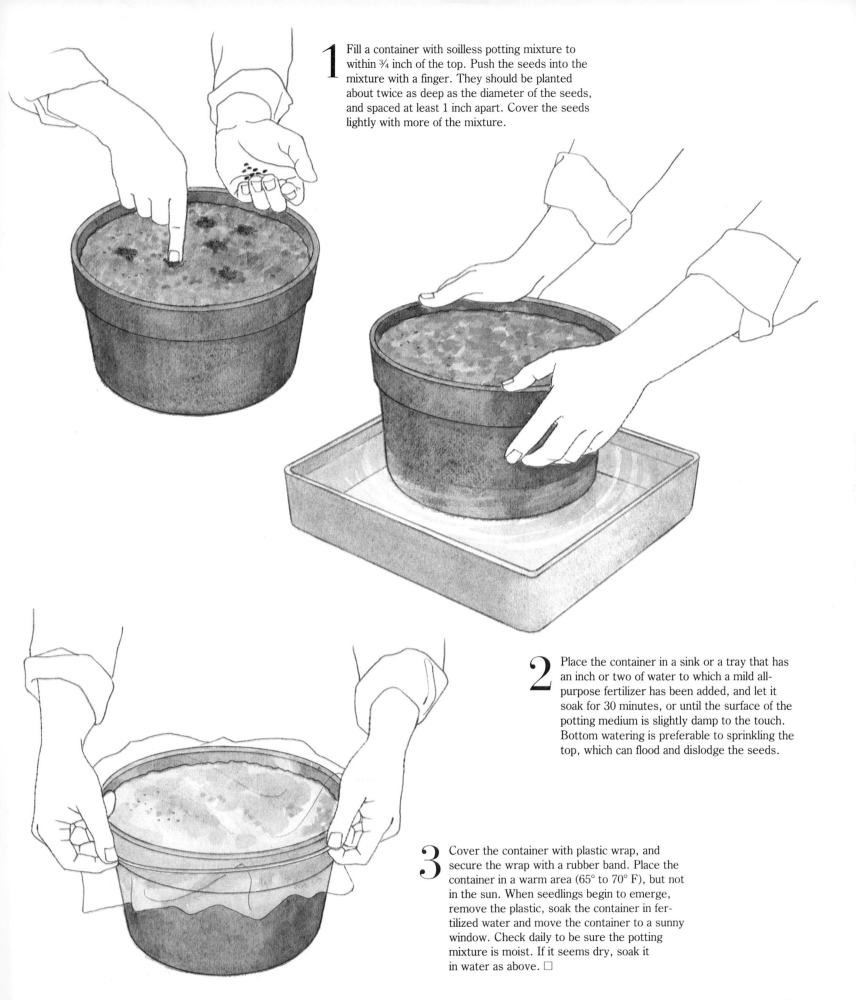

1 Fill a container with soilless potting mixture to within ¾ inch of the top. Push the seeds into the mixture with a finger. They should be planted about twice as deep as the diameter of the seeds, and spaced at least 1 inch apart. Cover the seeds lightly with more of the mixture.

2 Place the container in a sink or a tray that has an inch or two of water to which a mild all-purpose fertilizer has been added, and let it soak for 30 minutes, or until the surface of the potting medium is slightly damp to the touch. Bottom watering is preferable to sprinkling the top, which can flood and dislodge the seeds.

3 Cover the container with plastic wrap, and secure the wrap with a rubber band. Place the container in a warm area (65° to 70° F), but not in the sun. When seedlings begin to emerge, remove the plastic, soak the container in fertilized water and move the container to a sunny window. Check daily to be sure the potting mixture is moist. If it seems dry, soak it in water as above. □

MORE ROOM FOR YOUNG ROOTS

About three weeks after they stick their heads up, seedlings will grow a set of recognizably treelike leaves, as shown in the box on the opposite page. At this point the most vigorous of the young shoots should be selected, removed from their original containers and replanted in individual pots. The object is to give the roots plenty of space to develop, without being tangled together.

For transplanting, pots are essential because they provide more depth than trays. The pots can be made of peat, terra-cotta, plastic or metal. They must have holes in the bottom both for soak-style watering and the draining of excess moisture. And they must be large enough to accommodate the roots with growing room to spare.

The best planting medium is the same sort of soilless mixture used for sowing seeds *(pages 64-65)*. It should be kept moist and also fortified once a month with a mild solution of all-purpose fertilizer.

Tree seedlings should not be transplanted directly into the soil outdoors for one to three years; while they are small they may be run over by a lawn mower or trampled underfoot. But in the meantime they can be acclimated to outdoor conditions. At first, place the potted seedlings in a sunny area that is sheltered from wind for a few hours each warm day, and bring them indoors at night. Gradually increase the exposure until they can stay outdoors a full 24 hours. Then sink the pots into the ground to protect the roots from frost when fall comes. From time to time the plants will become root-bound and need to be dug up and transplanted to larger pots. With each transplanting, the pot size should be increased by 1 inch in diameter.

Three two-year-old dogwood seedlings, planted in pots, put out a healthy display of early-spring leaves. With another year's growth they will be big enough for transplanting into the ground.

STAGES OF GROWTH

Young tree seedlings develop at approximately the same rate as those of annuals and perennials begun indoors. They produce their first true leaves—the second pair to appear—in only 21 days. Their subsequent growth into mature plants, however, takes far longer. It takes a Chinese elm, pictured below, the better part of two years to attain a height of 24 inches and send out its first branches, and another year to reach 40 inches and produce subsidiary branches. The roots similarly establish themselves slowly, forming a solid 12-inch-deep base only after three years.

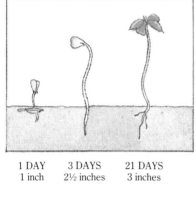

1 DAY	3 DAYS	21 DAYS
1 inch	2½ inches	3 inches

END OF FIRST
GROWING SEASON
10 inches

END OF SECOND
GROWING SEASON
24 inches

END OF THIRD
GROWING SEASON
40 inches

1 To begin transplanting tree seedlings into fresh, individual pots, tilt the original container and scoop out a clump of seedlings with your hand. Be sure to cradle the clump gently, and to include as much as possible of the planting mixture. Do not pull the seedlings up; pulling can both break the roots and bruise the stems.

2 Separate the seedlings carefully with your fingers, again leaving as much potting mixture around the roots as possible. Select the seedlings with the largest, greenest leaves and the most extensive root systems for transplanting. Throw away the weaker-looking ones; they will probably not develop into strong, thriving trees.

3 For each seedling you keep, fill a fresh pot to within ¾ inch of the top with planting mixture; then make a hole in the center with a piece of wood—an old pencil will do, or a chopstick. The hole needs to be deep and large enough to accommodate the root system.

4 Gently lower the seedling into the hole, holding it by the leaves, not the stem. Tamp the mixture around the seedling *(right)*. Only the roots should be covered. The point at which the stem and the roots meet should be flush with the surface of the mixture.

5 Place your container or containers in a tray of water 1 inch deep. Allow them to soak until the surface of the potting medium feels slightly damp. Move the pots to a sunny windowsill. Repeat the watering process whenever the potting soil begins to look and feel too dry. A daily check is a good idea, especially during warm weather. □

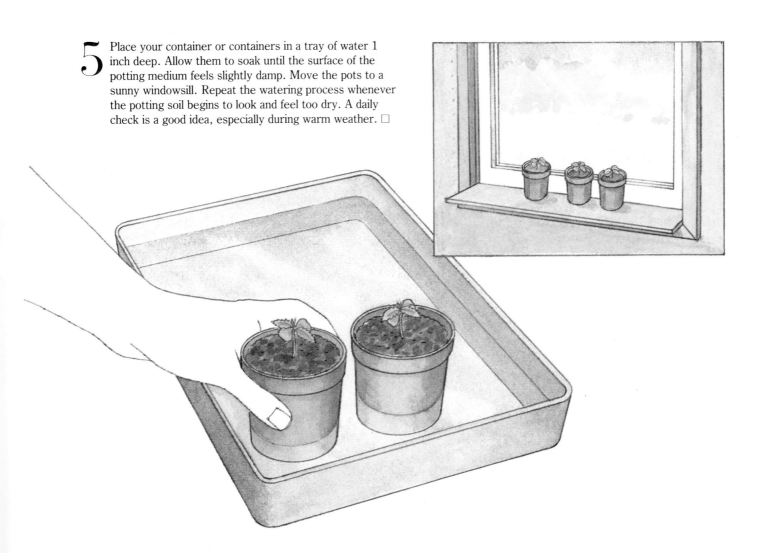

GROWING NEW TREES FROM STEM CUTTINGS

Their tops bathed in sunlight, three fig trees stand like sentinels along a fence. Figs are among the leafy trees that root most readily from cuttings.

The surest method of propagation—and one that bypasses some of the problems of seeds—is by means of softwood cuttings, the soft new shoots at the ends of branches that healthy trees produce in the spring. Softwood shoots can be snipped from dogwood, magnolia, weeping willow and many other deciduous trees, and from a variety of evergreens including hollies and yews. Cuttings should be made about two months after the shoots have begun to grow. If shoots first appear in mid-April, softwood cuttings from them can be taken in mid-July.

After cuttings have been growing in pots for two months, they will need to be transplanted into larger containers to relieve crowding. They should then be allowed to grow in their new containers until the end of their third season before being planted in the ground *(pages 8-11)*. They will need to be planted when dormant. Cuttings will survive best if the tree has recently absorbed water, either from rain or from sprinkling with a hose, and if they are made during the cool morning hours, not in the drying heat of midafternoon.

1 Select a few bright-leaved softwood stems and snip them off about 6 inches from the tip. Make the cut 1 inch below a node, where a leaf emerges from the stem, and cut at an angle *(inset)* so that you provide maximum stem surface for new roots to grow from.

2 Remove the leaves from the bottom two-thirds of each stem you have cut. Then roughen the bottom ½ inch of each cutting by scraping away the bark with a pair of shears or a knife. This will enable the cuttings to absorb moisture and nutrients and hasten the growing of roots.

3 Pour some of a hormone mixture that encourages rooting into a plastic bag. Dip the ends of the stems in the bag *(below),* making sure they get a thin, even coating. Do not dip the stems into your full supply of hormone mixture; any dampness will coagulate it, and any disease will contaminate it.

4 Plant the cuttings in a pot filled to within ¾ inch of the top with a planting mixture of peat moss and vermiculite. Space the cuttings 4 to 6 inches apart, and press them down so that the bottom leaves of each cutting are flush with the top of the potting mixture. Keep the mixture moist with regular but light waterings.

5 Push a pair of straight twigs (or chopsticks, dowels or old pencils) into the planting mixture. Put the pot in a large plastic bag, as shown, to keep moisture in. The wooden supports will keep the plastic away from the cuttings. The bagged pot should be kept outdoors if the weather is warm, but in indirect light; the shade of a grown tree will do.

6 Keep the cuttings in the plastic covering until new top growth is visible—probably in about two months. Then begin acclimating the new plants to the outdoor environment; for about a week, open the bag in the evenings and close it again during the warm daylight hours. After that, remove the plastic. □

ROOTING DECIDUOUS HARDWOOD STEMS

An alternative method is to cut hardwood stems in the winter, when the shoots have weathered a full growing season and are no longer soft. Curiously, hardwood cuttings from evergreens are planted in the same way as softwood shoots. But hardwood stems taken from deciduous trees must be 8 to 10 inches long and they require a storage period of about six weeks before planting. First, dip the stems in a rooting hormone powder and a fungicide. Then place them in a plastic bag and put the bag in the refrigerator.

After the storage period, put the cuttings in pots of planting mixture with only the top bud visible *(right);* this will secure the cuttings and in addition will prevent the buds from developing before the roots. Wrap the pots in plastic and keep them at 70° F. When the temperature turns warm outdoors, move the pots and acclimate the plants as explained above.

GRAFTING
WITH A LEAF BUD

Grafting is a man-made method of propagation in which parts of two separate plants are united to get the best properties of both. By means of it you can combine the beautiful blossoms of a delicate variety with the hardiness of another. Both trees must of course be healthy, and both should be of the same species; grafts of plants too different from each other seldom succeed. The tree to be used for the understock, or rootstock, should be a year-old seedling with a stem about ¼ to ½ inch in diameter.

There are a number of different methods of grafting. One of the simplest is bud grafting, which takes advantage of the growth potential locked inside a tiny leaf bud. All you do is cut off a tiny chip containing a leaf bud of the tree you wish to duplicate and attach it to a wound in the side of the stem of a rootstock of a hardier plant—deep enough for the cambium layers *(page 77)* of both plants to merge. Leaf buds are distinguishable from flower buds in that they are narrow and pointed; flower buds are round and plump.

Bud grafting can be done anytime, whether the trees are actively growing or dormant. But in warm weather, the graft should take effect in three to five weeks; if you do the grafting in fall, you won't see results until the following spring. The evidence that the graft has succeeded is the formation of a callus around the juncture of the two plant parts.

Since the new growth will resemble the bud stock in most respects, the appearance of the new tree will be determined by the placement of the graft. If you want the trunk to retain the bark of the understock, place the graft high up on the stem. If not, place it low; the understock will be cut off a few inches above the bud chip after the graft has taken.

The delicately hued blossoms of a row of crabapple trees form a canopy alongside a garden wall. Fruit trees are prime candidates for bud grafting because their flowers and fruits do not breed true from seed.

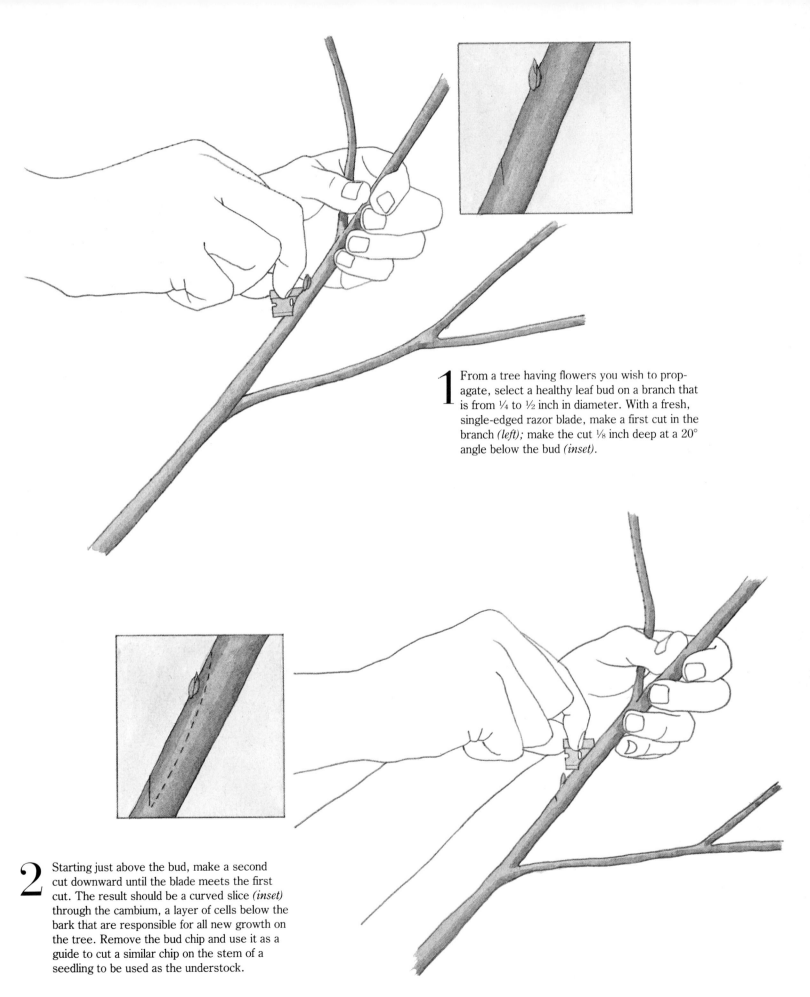

1 From a tree having flowers you wish to propagate, select a healthy leaf bud on a branch that is from ¼ to ½ inch in diameter. With a fresh, single-edged razor blade, make a first cut in the branch *(left)*; make the cut ⅛ inch deep at a 20° angle below the bud *(inset)*.

2 Starting just above the bud, make a second cut downward until the blade meets the first cut. The result should be a curved slice *(inset)* through the cambium, a layer of cells below the bark that are responsible for all new growth on the tree. Remove the bud chip and use it as a guide to cut a similar chip on the stem of a seedling to be used as the understock.

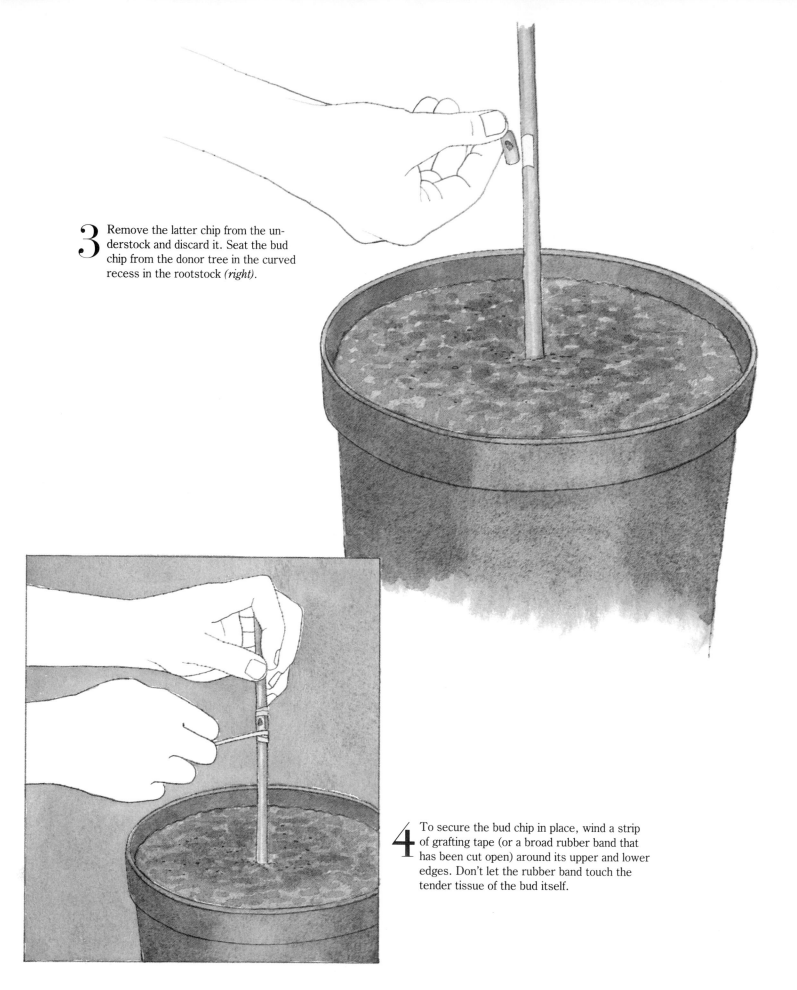

3 Remove the latter chip from the understock and discard it. Seat the bud chip from the donor tree in the curved recess in the rootstock *(right)*.

4 To secure the bud chip in place, wind a strip of grafting tape (or a broad rubber band that has been cut open) around its upper and lower edges. Don't let the rubber band touch the tender tissue of the bud itself.

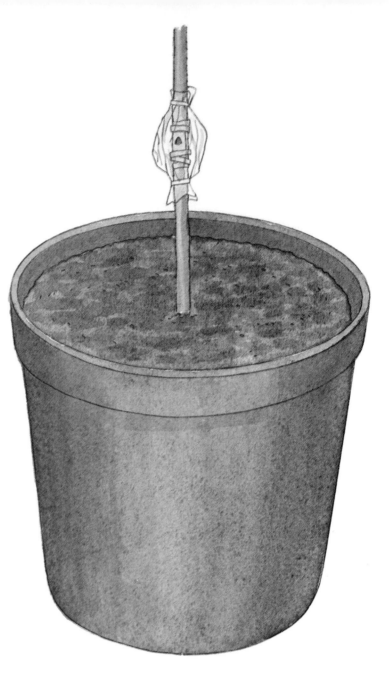

5 To keep the bud moist, cover the entire graft with clear plastic wrap and secure it with another pair of bands, one around the top and one around the bottom. In spring, when a callus has formed, remove the wrapping and the bands. Cut the top portion of the understock back to ½ inch above the grafted chip. The bud will soon blossom and grow to form the top of the new tree. □

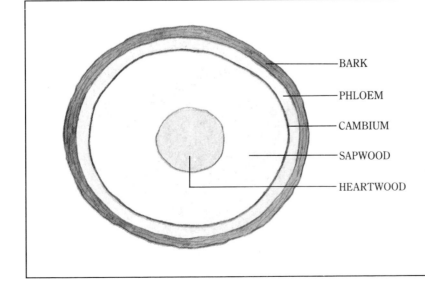

BARK

PHLOEM

CAMBIUM

SAPWOOD

HEARTWOOD

ANATOMY OF A TREE TRUNK

Beneath the bark that is visible are four layers of specialized tissue that are vital to the life of a tree. First comes an inner bark, called phloem, which carries newly synthesized organic material down from the leaves. Next comes the cambium layer, the generator of all new wood; one side produces phloem, the other side makes sapwood. The sapwood carries water and nutrients up from the roots to the leaves. At the core of the trunk is heartwood, which is inactive sapwood; it gives strength to the entire structure and stores foods and wastes. The merging of two cambium layers in a graft is necessary to the formation of a new plant.

JOINING A SHOOT TO A ROOTSTOCK

The big, bold flowers of a saucer magnolia put on a spectacular spring performance. You can multiply the pleasure this showy but tender bloomer provides by grafting a shoot of it onto a healthy rootstock of a related but hardier species.

Among the most common methods of grafting is scion grafting, in which a scion, or shoot, of one tree (called the donor tree) is joined atop the rootstock of another *(opposite and following pages)*. The key to the formation of a unified plant is the merging of the two trees' cambium *(box, page 77),* the layer of cells responsible for growth. Whether the trunk of the new tree will bear a stronger resemblance to the rootstock or to the scion depends on how much rootstock you retain below the graft. At a minimum, at least 2 to 3 inches of the rootstock stem must remain to support the scion.

Grafting should be done when both plants are dormant, so that they can become bonded together before either starts putting out new growth. It works best when both plants are of the same species; grafts between plants too different from one another rarely take. The scion and the rootstock should both be of the same diameter—usually, from ¼ to ½ inch. The rootstock should be a year-old seedling still being grown in its pot.

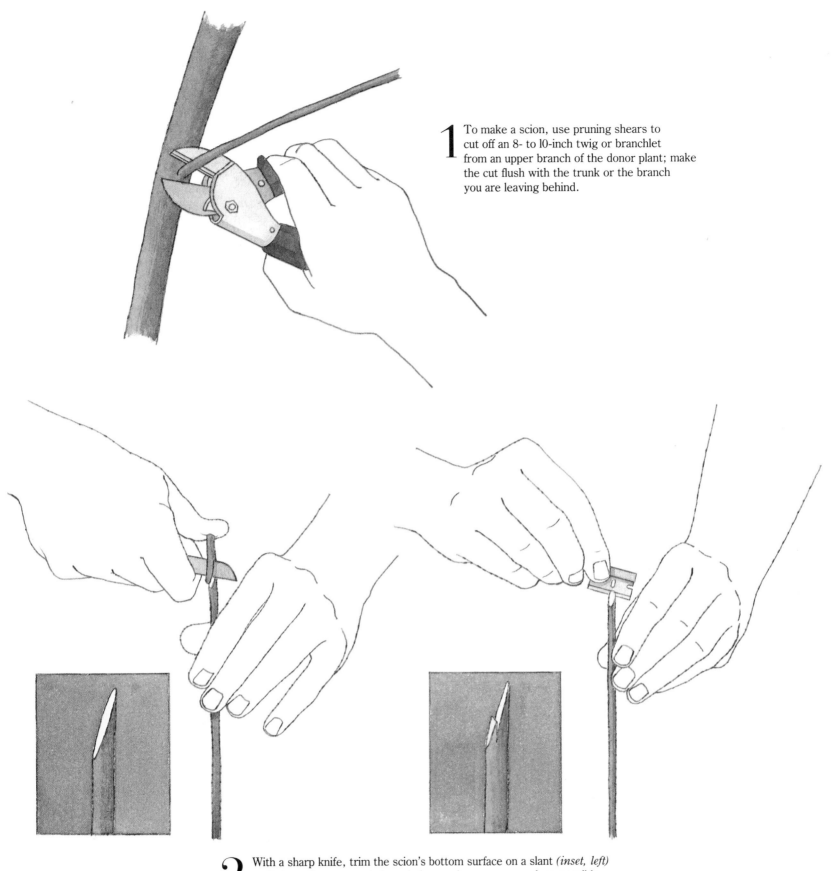

1 To make a scion, use pruning shears to cut off an 8- to 10-inch twig or branchlet from an upper branch of the donor plant; make the cut flush with the trunk or the branch you are leaving behind.

2 With a sharp knife, trim the scion's bottom surface on a slant *(inset, left)* so that you form an oval-shaped plane and expose as much as possible of the cambium layer beneath the bark. Then, holding the stem steady with one hand and using a single-edged razor blade with the other, make a neat incision in the bottom surface of the scion, pressing straight down to a depth of ¼ inch. Do not remove any wood. The result should be a tongue and groove *(inset, right)*.

3 With pruning shears, cut off the top of the rootstock plant; make the cut about 1 inch above a bud and leave the stem of the rootstock at least 2 to 3 inches tall *(left)*. Then place a sharp knife just above the bud and cut upward at a slant across the stem so that you have an oval-shaped plane, as with the scion in Step 2. Make sure the cut is at an angle that will fit against the bottom surface of the scion; then cut a matching ¼-inch tongue and groove in the slanted oval upper surface of the rootstock.

4 Holding the rootstock stem steady with one hand, use the other hand to join the scion and the rootstock together so that the tongues lock in the opposing grooves *(inset)*.

5 To keep the graft immobilized while a callus forms, bind the scion and the rootstock together with a rubber band that you have cut open or with a length of grafting tape (sold at garden centers). Wind the band around the graft, stretching it as tight as possible. To lock it in place, hold open the last loop with one finger, pull the end through the loop and let the band snap down on itself.

6 Water the newly grafted tree, cover it and the pot with a plastic bag, and tie the bag shut. Store the plant in a dark place at 40° to 50° F for at least two months. At the end of that time, expose the plant to outside air gradually; open the plastic bag for a few hours every day for about a week, then take the bag off and move the plant into the light. For another few days, acclimate it to the outdoors, a few hours per day; then the new tree may be transplanted into the ground. After about a year, use a razor blade to slice off the rubber band so that it will not constrict the growing stem. □

5
MAKING THE MOST OF NATURE

Since the life of a healthy tree is measured in decades and even centuries, trees are natural symbols of endurance. But a tree out of place may not survive at all, and one neglected will never reach its full potential. Before planting a tree, therefore, you will find it useful to consult the Zone Map on pages 84-85, which indicates the 10 climate zones, based on the coldest winter temperatures, into which the United States Department of Agriculture divides the country. Note the zone you live in; then turn to the Dictionary of Trees to find out which varieties are likely to flourish in your area.

Even the healthiest trees can use help in withstanding extremes of weather and seasonal challenges. The checklist on pages 86-89 tells you what steps to take, month by month, to maintain your trees at the peak of condition.

Starting on page 90 is a veritable rogues' gallery of pests and diseases that may threaten your trees. The entries are keyed to common danger signs such as loss of vigor, branch dieback and leaf discoloration. In each case, detailed information is provided to help you identify the problem and take swift corrective action.

Finally, there is a section of tips designed to help you get the most out of your trees. Included are suggestions for safety when planting, preventing ornamental trees from forming unwanted fruit and creating unusual visual effects by giving your trees a European "haircut."

THE ZONE MAP AND PLANTING

When choosing a tree for your garden, there's more to consider than height, shape, flowers and foliage. One of the most important considerations is how well the tree can adapt to the climate of the zone in which you live. Climate has an effect on several aspects of a tree's development. It determines not only whether a tree can survive, but also how large it will grow. It may even determine whether a tree will be deciduous or evergreen. Some trees, such as Chinese elms *(page 136),* are evergreen in the warm regions of southern California, but deciduous in the cold winter areas of northern Vermont. Other trees, such as cherries *(page 128),* need winter frost in order to produce flowers and foliage in spring. To find out how a particular tree will fare in your zone, consult the Dictionary of Trees *(pages 96-137).*

To determine which zone you live in, look at the map at right. The zones have been established by the U.S. Department of Agriculture, which divides North America into 10 climatic areas. The zones are determined by minimum winter temperatures. Zone 1 is the coldest, with winter lows of −50° F. Zone 10 is the warmest; it rarely experiences frost and its minimum winter temperatures seldom drop lower than 30° F.

Both the regions on the map and the temperatures should be used only as guidelines. Temperatures of adjacent zones are similar at their boundary lines. And within any given zone, temperatures can vary from year to year by five or more degrees.

With a little help, some trees can be grown in the zones that border their recommended zones. A tree such as iigiri *(page 116),* which is only marginally hardy in Zone 7, can survive in that zone if it is located in a protected spot, such as on the south side of a house or by a wall where it will receive the warmth of the sun.

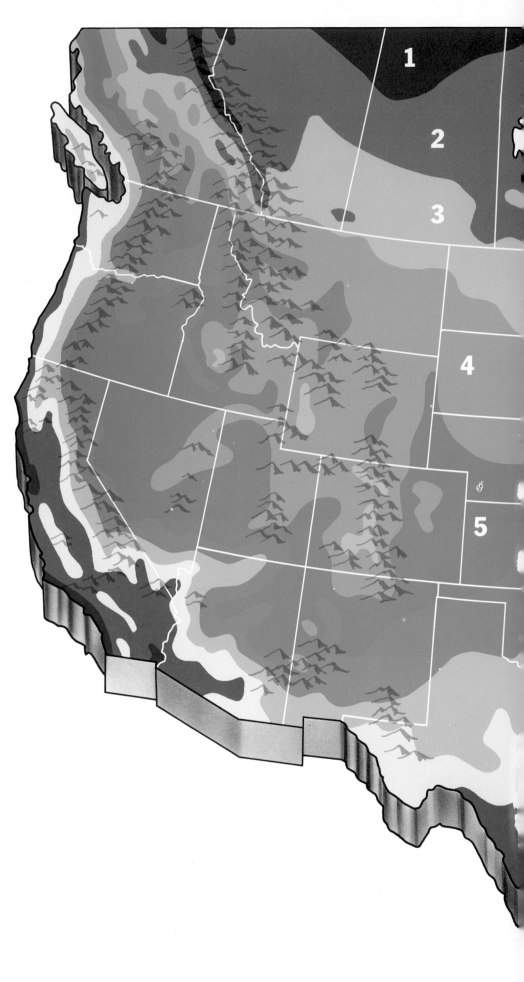

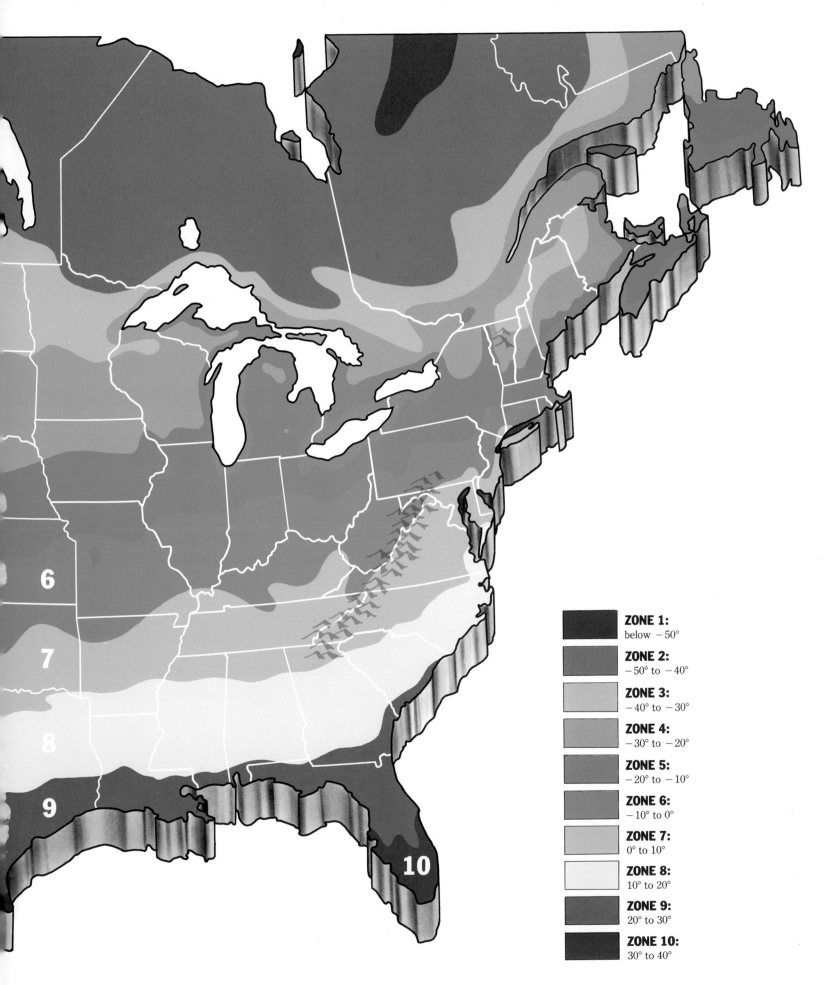

6

7

8

9

10

	ZONE 1: below −50°
	ZONE 2: −50° to −40°
	ZONE 3: −40° to −30°
	ZONE 4: −30° to −20°
	ZONE 5: −20° to −10°
	ZONE 6: −10° to 0°
	ZONE 7: 0° to 10°
	ZONE 8: 10° to 20°
	ZONE 9: 20° to 30°
	ZONE 10: 30° to 40°

A CHECKLIST FOR MAINTENANCE MONTH BY MONTH

	ZONE 1	ZONE 2	ZONE 3	ZONE 4	ZONE 5
JANUARY/FEBRUARY	• Prune dormant trees • Spray evergreens with antidesiccant • Remove snow and ice from evergreens after every snowfall • Replace mulch as needed	• Prune dormant trees • Spray evergreens with antidesiccant • Remove snow and ice from evergreens after every snowfall • Replace mulch as needed	• Prune dormant trees • Spray evergreens with antidesiccant • Remove snow and ice from evergreens after every snowfall • Replace mulch as needed	• Prune dormant trees • Spray evergreens with antidesiccant • Remove snow and ice from evergreens after every snowfall • Replace mulch as needed	• Prune dormant trees • Spray evergreens with antidesiccant • Remove snow and ice from evergreens after every snowfall • Replace mulch as needed
MARCH/APRIL	• Clean, oil, sharpen tools	• Clean, oil, sharpen tools	• Clean, oil, sharpen tools	• Plant bare-root trees • Plant container and balled-and-burlapped trees • Apply horticultural oil • Clean, oil, sharpen tools	• Prune out winter damage • Plant bare-root trees • Plant container and balled-and-burlapped trees • Remove winter mulch and burlap wrappings • Apply horticultural oil • Clean, oil, sharpen tools
MAY/JUNE	• Prune trees • Prune out winter damage • Shear fine-needled evergreens • Fertilize trees as growth starts • Plant bare-root trees • Plant container and balled-and-burlapped trees • Transplant trees • Remove winter mulch and burlap wrappings • Apply horticultural oil • Weed soil around trees; apply pre-emergent herbicide • Apply summer mulch • Check for insects, diseases	• Prune trees • Prune out winter damage • Shear fine-needled evergreens • Fertilize trees as growth starts • Plant bare-root trees • Plant container and balled-and-burlapped trees • Transplant trees • Remove winter mulch and burlap wrappings • Apply horticultural oil • Weed soil around trees; apply pre-emergent herbicide • Apply summer mulch • Check for insects, diseases	• Prune trees • Prune out winter damage • Shear fine-needled evergreens • Fertilize trees as growth starts • Plant bare-root trees • Plant container and balled-and-burlapped trees • Transplant trees • Remove winter mulch and burlap wrappings • Apply horticultural oil • Weed soil around trees; apply pre-emergent herbicide • Apply summer mulch • Check for insects, diseases	• Prune trees • Prune out winter damage • Shear fine-needled evergreens • Fertilize trees as growth starts • Plant bare-root trees • Plant container and balled-and-burlapped trees • Transplant trees • Remove winter mulch and burlap wrappings • Weed soil around trees; apply pre-emergent herbicide • Apply summer mulch • Check for insects, diseases	• Prune trees • Shear fine-needled evergreens • Fertilize trees as growth starts • Plant container and balled-and-burlapped trees • Transplant trees • Weed soil around trees; apply pre-emergent herbicide • Apply summer mulch • Water as necessary • Check for insects, diseases

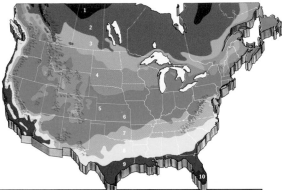

	ZONE 6	ZONE 7	ZONE 8	ZONE 9	ZONE 10	
	• Prune dormant trees • Spray evergreens with antidesiccant • Remove snow and ice from evergreens after every snowfall • Replace mulch as needed • Clean, oil, sharpen tools	• Prune dormant trees • Spray evergreens with antidesiccant • Remove snow and ice from evergreens after every snowfall • Replace mulch as needed • Clean, oil, sharpen tools	• Prune trees • Fertilize trees as growth starts • Plant bare-root trees • Plant container and balled-and-burlapped trees • Remove winter mulch and burlap wrappings • Apply horticultural oil • Clean, oil, sharpen tools	• Prune trees • Fertilize trees as growth starts • Plant bare-root trees • Plant container and balled-and-burlapped trees • Transplant trees • Apply horticultural oil • Water if ground is dry • Check for insects, diseases • Clean, oil, sharpen tools	• Prune trees • Fertilize trees as growth starts • Plant bare-root trees • Plant container and balled-and-burlapped trees • Transplant trees • Apply horticultural oil • Water if ground is dry • Check for insects, diseases • Clean, oil, sharpen tools	JANUARY/FEBRUARY
	• Prune trees • Prune out winter damage • Fertilize trees as growth starts • Plant bare-root trees • Plant container and balled-and-burlapped trees • Transplant trees • Remove winter mulch and burlap wrappings • Apply horticultural oil	• Prune trees • Prune out winter damage • Fertilize trees as growth starts • Plant bare-root trees • Plant container and balled-and-burlapped trees • Transplant trees • Remove winter mulch and burlap wrappings • Apply horticultural oil	• Prune trees • Prune out winter damage • Shear fine-needled evergreens • Fertilize trees as growth starts • Plant container and balled-and-burlapped trees • Transplant trees • Weed soil around trees; apply pre-emergent herbicide • Apply summer mulch • Water if ground is dry • Check for insects, diseases	• Shear fine-needled evergreens • Plant container and balled-and-burlapped trees • Weed soil around trees; apply pre-emergent herbicide • Apply summer mulch • Water if ground is dry • Check for insects, diseases	• Shear fine-needled evergreens • Plant container and balled-and-burlapped trees • Weed soil around trees; apply pre-emergent herbicide • Apply summer mulch • Water if ground is dry • Check for insects, diseases	MARCH/APRIL
	• Prune trees • Shear fine-needled evergreens • Plant container and balled-and-burlapped trees • Transplant trees • Weed soil around trees; apply pre-emergent herbicide • Apply summer mulch • Water as necessary • Check for insects, diseases	• Prune trees • Shear fine-needled evergreens • Plant container and balled-and-burlapped trees • Transplant trees • Weed soil around trees; apply pre-emergent herbicide • Apply summer mulch • Water as necessary • Check for insects, diseases	• Prune trees • Shear fine-needled evergreens • Plant container and balled-and-burlapped trees • Weed beds around trees; apply pre-emergent herbicide • Apply summer mulch • Water as necessary • Check for insects, diseases	• Shear fine-needled evergreens • Plant container and balled-and-burlapped trees • Weed soil around trees; apply pre-emergent herbicide • Apply summer mulch • Water as necessary • Check for insects, diseases	• Shear fine-needled evergreens • Plant container and balled-and-burlapped trees • Weed soil around trees; apply pre-emergent herbicide • Apply summer mulch • Water as necessary • Check for insects, diseases	MAY/JUNE

	ZONE 1	ZONE 2	ZONE 3	ZONE 4	ZONE 5
JULY/AUGUST	• Shear fine-needled evergreens • Plant container and balled-and-burlapped trees • Transplant evergreen trees • Weed soil around trees; apply pre-emergent herbicide • Aerate compacted soil around roots • Take cuttings for propagation • Water as necessary • Check for insects, diseases	• Shear fine-needled evergreens • Plant container and balled-and-burlapped trees • Transplant evergreen trees • Weed soil around trees; apply pre-emergent herbicide • Aerate compacted soil around roots • Take cuttings for propagation • Water as necessary • Check for insects, diseases	• Shear fine-needled evergreens • Plant container and balled-and-burlapped trees • Transplant evergreen trees • Weed soil around trees; apply pre-emergent herbicide • Aerate compacted soil around roots • Take cuttings for propagation • Water as necessary • Check for insects, diseases	• Shear fine-needled evergreens • Plant container and balled-and-burlapped trees • Transplant evergreen trees • Weed soil around trees; apply pre-emergent herbicide • Aerate compacted soil around roots • Take cuttings for propagation • Water as necessary • Check for insects, diseases	• Shear fine-needled evergreens • Plant container and balled-and-burlapped trees • Weed soil around trees; apply pre-emergent herbicide • Aerate compacted soil around roots • Water as necessary • Check for insects, diseases
SEPTEMBER/OCTOBER	• Plant container and balled-and-burlapped deciduous trees • Transplant deciduous trees • Water if ground is dry • Rake leaves • Apply winter mulch and wrap tree trunks in burlap • Turn off water, drain hose	• Plant container and balled-and-burlapped deciduous trees • Transplant deciduous trees • Rake leaves • Water if ground is dry • Apply winter mulch and wrap tree trunks in burlap • Turn off water, drain hose	• Plant container and balled-and-burlapped deciduous trees • Transplant deciduous trees • Water if ground is dry • Rake leaves • Apply winter mulch and wrap tree trunks in burlap • Turn off water, drain hose	• Plant container and balled-and-burlapped deciduous trees • Transplant deciduous trees • Water if ground is dry • Rake leaves • Apply winter mulch and wrap tree trunks in burlap • Turn off water, drain hose	• Plant container and balled-and-burlapped trees • Transplant deciduous and evergreen trees • Take cuttings for propagation • Water if ground is dry • Rake leaves
NOVEMBER/DECEMBER	• Prune dormant trees • Fertilize dormant trees • Spray evergreens with antidesiccant • Put wire mesh around trunks for protection against animals • Remove snow and ice from evergreens after every snowfall	• Prune dormant trees • Fertilize dormant trees • Spray evergreens with antidesiccant • Put wire mesh around trunks for protection against animals • Remove snow and ice from evergreens after every snowfall	• Prune dormant trees • Fertilize dormant trees • Spray evergreens with antidesiccant • Put wire mesh around trunks for protection against animals • Remove snow and ice from evergreens after every snowfall	• Prune dormant trees • Fertilize dormant trees • Spray evergreens with antidesiccant • Put wire mesh around trunks for protection against animals • Remove snow and ice from evergreens after every snowfall	• Prune dormant trees • Fertilize dormant trees • Spray evergreens with antidesiccant • Apply winter mulch and wrap tree trunks in burlap • Put wire mesh around trunks for protection against animals • Remove snow and ice from evergreens after every snowfall • Water if ground is dry • Turn off water, drain hose • Rake leaves

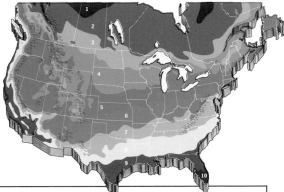

	ZONE 6	ZONE 7	ZONE 8	ZONE 9	ZONE 10	
	• Shear fine-needled evergreens • Plant container and balled-and-burlapped trees • Weed soil around trees; apply pre-emergent herbicide • Aerate compacted soil around roots • Water as necessary • Check for insects, diseases	• Shear fine-needled evergreens • Plant container and balled-and-burlapped trees • Weed soil around trees; apply pre-emergent herbicide • Aerate compacted soil around roots • Water as necessary • Check for insects, diseases	• Shear fine-needled evergreens • Plant container and balled-and-burlapped trees • Weed soil around trees; apply pre-emergent herbicide • Aerate compacted soil around roots • Water as necessary • Check for insects, diseases	• Shear fine-needled evergreens • Plant container and balled-and-burlapped trees • Weed soil around trees; apply pre-emergent herbicide • Aerate compacted soil around roots • Water as necessary • Check for insects, diseases	• Shear fine-needled evergreens • Plant container and balled-and-burlapped trees • Weed soil around trees; apply pre-emergent herbicide • Aerate compacted soil around roots • Water as necessary • Check for insects, diseases	**JULY/AUGUST**
	• Plant container and balled-and-burlapped trees • Transplant evergreen trees • Take cuttings for propagation • Water if ground is dry • Rake leaves	• Plant container and balled-and-burlapped trees • Transplant evergreen trees • Take cuttings for propagation • Water if ground is dry • Rake leaves	• Plant container and balled-and-burlapped trees • Transplant evergreen trees • Take cuttings for propagation • Water if ground is dry • Rake leaves	• Plant container and balled-and-burlapped trees • Transplant evergreen trees • Take cuttings for propagation • Water if ground is dry • Rake leaves	• Plant container and balled-and-burlapped trees • Transplant evergreen trees • Take cuttings for propagation • Water if ground is dry • Rake leaves	**SEPTEMBER/OCTOBER**
	• Prune dormant trees • Fertilize dormant trees • Plant bare-root trees • Transplant deciduous trees • Spray evergreens with antidesiccant • Apply winter mulch and wrap tree trunks in burlap • Put wire mesh around trunks for protection against animals • Water if ground is dry • Turn off water, drain hose • Rake leaves	• Prune dormant trees • Fertilize dormant trees • Plant container and balled-and-burlapped trees • Plant bare-root trees • Transplant deciduous trees • Spray evergreens with antidesiccant • Apply winter mulch and wrap tree trunks in burlap • Put wire mesh around trunks for protection against animals • Take cuttings for propagation • Water if ground is dry • Turn off water, drain hose • Rake leaves	• Prune dormant trees • Fertilize dormant trees • Plant container and balled-and-burlapped trees • Plant bare-root trees • Transplant deciduous trees • Spray evergreens with antidesiccant • Apply winter mulch and wrap tree trunks in burlap • Put wire mesh around trunks for protection against animals • Take cuttings for propagation • Water if ground is dry • Turn off water, drain hose • Rake leaves	• Prune trees • Fertilize dormant trees • Plant container and balled-and-burlapped trees • Transplant deciduous trees • Take cuttings for propagation • Water if ground is dry • Rake leaves	• Prune trees • Fertilize dormant trees • Plant container and balled-and-burlapped trees • Plant bare-root trees • Transplant deciduous trees • Take cuttings for propagation • Water if ground is dry • Rake leaves	**NOVEMBER/DECEMBER**

WHAT TO DO
WHEN THINGS GO WRONG

PROBLEM	CAUSE	SOLUTION
Trees lose their foliage in late spring. Translucent egg clusters several inches in diameter may be seen on the tree trunks. Many trees, including birch, elm, hawthorn, linden, maple, oak, pine, poplar and willow may be affected.	Gypsy moth caterpillars, which are 2 inches long and have hairy brown bodies with red spots.	Scrape egg clusters off trunks and destroy them. Spray caterpillars with an insecticide or *Bacillus thuringiensis,* called Bt, a bacterium fatal to caterpillars but harmless to plants and other animals. Tie a piece of burlap around each affected trunk; the caterpillars will be trapped under the burlap and can then be collected and destroyed.
Leaves curl, buds and flowers are deformed, and tree growth is stunted. Leaves may be coated with a black, sooty powder. Beech, birch, crabapple, elm, flowering fruit, linden, maple, oak, pine and willow trees are susceptible.	Aphids, ⅛-inch, semitransparent insects that may be green, yellow, black, brown or red. Aphids carry bacterial, fungal and viral diseases.	In early spring, before the leaf buds open, spray the foliage with horticultural oil, which smothers insects and their eggs. Treat infestations as they appear with an insecticide. Repeat applications at one-week intervals, if necessary.
Silky, weblike nests that resemble tents appear in the crotches of birch, elm, flowering fruit, hawthorn, maple, oak, poplar and willow trees. Caterpillars may be visible on the foliage during the day.	Tent caterpillars, hairy, 2-inch-long insects with blue spots and red stripes.	Spray with an insecticide or *Bacillus thuringiensis,* called Bt, a bacterium fatal to caterpillars but harmless to plants and other animals.
Trees cease to grow and may die. White, cottony patches and small, brown round or oval shells appear on branches, twigs, and sometimes leaves and fruit. Any tree may be affected.	Any of a number of scale insects, from ⅒ to ⅜ inch long, with gray, white, yellow, green, black, brown, red or purple shells. The cottony patches are egg sacs.	In midspring, spray with horticultural oil, which will smother the eggs and young insects. Treat infestations as they appear with an insecticide. Repeat applications at one-week intervals, if necessary.
Upper surfaces of leaves lose color and are covered with white or yellow speckles; undersides of leaves are covered with small, dark specks. Susceptible trees are ash, birch, elm, hawthorn, hickory, linden, oak, sycamore, walnut and willow.	Lace bugs, tiny flat bugs ¹⁄₁₆ to ⅛ inch long with transparent, lacy wings and hoodlike coverings on their heads.	Spray with an insecticide in midspring and again in midsummer to control successive generations of lace bugs, which mature in six to eight weeks.
Cocoonlike, 1- to 2-inch bags that look like brown, dry foliage hang from branches. The most susceptible trees are conifers such as hemlock, juniper, larch and pine, but linden, locust and maple can also be affected.	Bagworm, a 1-inch caterpillar with a brown or black body and a white or yellow head. It uses pieces of leaves and twigs to construct a bag around itself.	In winter or spring, the bags may be handpicked and destroyed before the caterpillars emerge. In late spring or early summer, when caterpillars emerge, apply an insecticide or *Bacillus thuringiensis,* called Bt, a bacterium fatal to caterpillars but harmless to plants and other animals.

PROBLEM	CAUSE	SOLUTION
Trees become defoliated. Eggs appear on the undersides and the bases of the leaves. Both evergreen and deciduous trees are susceptible.	Sawfly larvae, caterpillar-like insects 1 to 1½ inches long. Most are green, with stripes or spots, and resemble the needlelike foliage of conifers.	Spray with an insecticide when the insects appear in late spring. Repeat applications may be needed to control successive generations.
Bark on lower sections of trunks is missing or ragged.	Deer, rabbit or other animals.	Tree trunks can be wrapped in burlap or encased in cylinders of wire mesh or tar paper. Protection should reach 20 inches higher than the average snowfall line.
Light green or brown serpentine markings appear on leaves; leaves eventually turn brown and die. Some species of birch are susceptible; so are aspen, crabapple, elm, flowering fruit, hawthorn, holly, locust, oak, pine, spruce and tupelo trees.	Leaf miners, which are the larvae of flies, moths or beetles that tunnel into leaf surfaces.	Spray with a systemic pesticide in spring. Apply pesticide to the ground out to the drip line under infested trees. If the infestation is severe, consult a professional arborist.
Irregular holes appear in leaves of elm and other shade trees. Eventually, entire trees may be defoliated.	Beetles, including the Japanese beetle, a ½-inch, metallic green insect; the larva of the elm leaf beetle, a ½-inch yellow grub striped or spotted with black; and the elm bark beetle, which is ⅛ inch long and reddish brown.	Adult forms of beetles can be controlled with insecticide. Larvae should be controlled with insecticides applied to trees and to the lawn around trees. Spraying for a second generation five to six weeks later may also be necessary.
Trees are suddenly defoliated. Insects can be seen hanging from branches on thin, silklike threads. Beech, elm and other shade trees may be affected.	Cankerworm, also called inchworm, a ½-inch moth larva that is usually green, but may be brown or black. Larvae can be identified by the way they arch their backs as they move.	Spray with an insecticide or *Bacillus thuringiensis,* called Bt, a bacterium fatal to caterpillars but harmless to plants and other animals. In an area having a history of infestation by the pest, spray in early spring before the insect appears.
Leaves lose their color and upper leaf surfaces take on a dull silver or bronze sheen. Tiny black specks and small translucent blisters may be seen on the undersides of leaves. Eventually, leaves wither and drop and webs may appear on branches. Juniper, linden, locust, maple, mountain ash, oak, pine and walnut are susceptible.	One of a number of mites, microscopic spiderlike pests.	Spray with horticultural oil in spring before leaf buds open. If symptoms appear in summer, apply a miticide. Repeat applications three days apart are usually necessary for control.
Leaves are small or sparse. Tree growth slows or stops. Small round holes may appear in the bark. Dogwood is particularly susceptible, but ash, birch, cottonwood, elm, hemlock, honey locust, linden, locust, maple, oak, pine and poplar are also susceptible.	Borers, ½- to 2½-inch-long caterpillars that work their way into the bark and destroy the tree from inside the trunk.	Stressed trees are particularly vulnerable to borer attack, so keep trees well watered, fertilized and disease-free. Wrap paper or plastic around the tree trunks to discourage borers. Once they have entered the trunk, they can be cut out with a knife if they are near the surface. An insecticide may be applied to the bark where holes appear.

PROBLEM	CAUSE	SOLUTION
Leaves at the ends of branches suddenly wilt, turn black and appear to have been scorched by fire. Twigs may also turn black. Dark brown cankers several inches long develop on trunks and main branches. Crabapple, flowering fruit, hawthorn and mountain ash trees are susceptible.	Fire blight, a bacterial disease.	There are no chemical controls. Prune out damaged branches and disinfect pruning tools with alcohol after each cut. Spray with an antibiotic every five to seven days when the trees are in bloom to prevent the disease.
Leaves are distorted in shape, turn yellow and drop. Leaves and twigs are covered with a whitish gray powder. Symptoms are most severe when days are warm and nights are cool. Many deciduous trees can be affected.	Powdery mildew, a fungal disease.	To prevent or control the disease, spray with a fungicide once a week during periods of warm days and cool nights.
Leaves on one branch, several branches or an entire tree first turn yellow, then brown, wilt and may drop. A cross section of a branch reveals a dark ring or rings. Maples are the most susceptible, but many types of trees can be affected.	Verticillium wilt, a fungal disease. Its presence can be confirmed only by a laboratory test of a damaged branch.	There are no chemical controls. Remove damaged tree parts. If infection is severe, the tree cannot be saved and must be removed to prevent the spread of the disease.
Small brown spots form on new leaves and spread until entire leaves are brown and look scorched. Leaves drop and are succeeded by a set of healthy leaves. If this occurs in successive years, the trees will become stressed and may die. Ash, linden, maple, oak and sycamore may be affected.	Anthracnose, a fungal disease that is particularly severe in wet weather because the fungus is spread by splashing water.	A fungicide can be used both to prevent and to control the disease. Spray in spring when leaf buds start to open and repeat two or three times, 10 to 14 days apart. Destroy all fallen leaves.
Rough, round swellings up to several inches across appear on tree trunks, branches and roots. Trees may cease to grow, leaves may yellow and branches may die back. Young trees may die. Susceptible trees are chestnut, flowering fruit, juniper, oak, poplar, sycamore, walnut and willow.	Crown gall, a bacterial disease that inhabits the soil.	There are no chemical controls. Prune out damaged branches on affected trees. Do not plant susceptible trees in an area with a history of the disease.
Areas between the veins or along the margins of leaves turn white, brown or yellow. Leaves may also be speckled or streaked or have a silvery sheen.	Air pollution.	There are no controls for pollution. Pollution-tolerant trees are available, such as Carolina poplar, elm, gingko, linden, Norway maple, pin oak, sycamore, tree-of-heaven and tulip tree.
Red, brown or black patches appear on stems, branches and trunks. Infected areas expand and eventually may kill the tree.	Canker, a fungal or bacterial disease.	Stressed trees are particularly susceptible to canker, so keep trees well watered, fertilized and free of insects. Prune out infected parts as soon as they appear and disinfect tools with alcohol after each cut. If infection is severe, the tree must be removed to prevent the spread of the disease.

PROBLEM	CAUSE	SOLUTION
Yellow spots appear on upper surfaces of leaves, and the undersides are covered with a reddish orange dust. Crabapple, hawthorn, juniper, pine, poplar and red cedar trees are susceptible. When a juniper is infected, red or green galls form on the stems and leaves. When a pine is infected, small cankers appear on the trunk and branches *(right)*.	Rust, a fungal disease.	Rust develops only when certain plants are grown near each other, and these combinations should be avoided. Do not plant pine trees near gooseberry or currant. Do not plant crabapple or hawthorn near red cedar or juniper. Do not plant poplar trees near hemlock. If symptoms appear, spray with a fungicide three times, 10 days apart.
Leaves at the tops of trees and toward the ends of long branches begin to droop and lose their color and shine. Young trees are especially susceptible.	Insufficient water.	Check the soil in the upper 12 inches around the base of an affected tree. If the soil is so dry that it crumbles in your hand, the tree needs water. Soak thoroughly and apply mulch to help retain moisture.
Small, round dark spots, sometimes surrounded by yellow rings, appear on leaves. As the spots expand in size, the entire leaves become dark and usually drop. Catalpa, dogwood, elm, flowering fruit, hawthorn, hickory, oak and walnut trees are susceptible.	Leaf spot, caused by a number of fungi or bacteria. The disease is particularly severe in wet weather because the fungi and bacteria are spread by splashing water.	Rake and destroy all fallen leaves. A fungicide can be used both to prevent and to control leaf spot. Spray once every 10 days, four times, starting when leaf buds begin to open.
Malodorous sap flows from wounds in bark. The sap may be either brown or white and foamy. Birch, elm, maple, oak, poplar, sycamore and willow are susceptible.	Slime flux, a bacterial infection. The bacteria enter the tree through wounds caused by injury, such as lawn-mower cuts or from insects, and then they infect the sap.	There are no chemical controls for slime flux. Paint wounds with tree-wound paint. Drill a hole slanted upward into the tree just below the wound and insert a plastic tube into the hole; this will allow infected sap to drain away from the tree and promote healing of the wound.
Leaves wilt and drop. Branches stop growing and may die. A white, fan-shaped fungal growth appears just under the bark near the base of the tree or just under the soil line. Eventually, long, round black strands of tissue form under the bark and on or near the roots. Many trees are susceptible.	Shoestring root rot, a fungal disease.	Stressed trees are particularly susceptible to shoestring root rot, so keep trees well watered, fertilized and free of insects and diseases. Remove the damaged parts of partially infected trees. If the entire root system is infected, the tree must be removed and the soil around it replaced.
Leaf edges appear scorched. Fall coloration of leaves occurs prematurely in summer, and leaves drop. Trees along roadways and footpaths are the most susceptible.	Salt injury. This occurs when roots take in salt applied to the ground to melt ice and snow.	Use sand or sawdust instead of salt. Plant salt-tolerant trees, such as black birch, black cherry, black locust, gray birch, paper birch, red cedar, red oak, white ash, white oak or yellow birch along roadways.

TIPS AND TECHNIQUES

BRINGING OUTDOOR FRAGRANCE INDOORS

The fresh scents of the forest can add charm to your yard and to your house. Several broad-leaved evergreens, such as bay laurel and eucalyptus, and many conifers, such as balsam, cedar, fir and pine, have bark and foliage with long-lasting fragrance.

To bring these scents indoors, you can make sachets filled with scraps of aromatic bark and foliage, and spread them around your house.

Some tree fragrances also repel insects. Aromatic cedar bark placed in closets and drawers will help keep moths away from woolens. Redwood bark used as a mulch can keep many crawling insects, such as caterpillars, out of planting beds in the garden.

PREVENTING FRUIT FORMATION

Many gardeners want to enjoy the beauty of blossoming fruit trees without the fruit that follows the flowers. Fruit creates time-consuming cleanup chores; it drops on lawns, patios and paths, and sometimes clogs sewer drains. And a few fruits, such as those of the female ginkgo tree, are undesirable because of their unpleasant odor.

There are two ways to prevent fruit from forming. The first is to spray trees with an antidesiccant when the flowers begin to open. This seals the flower surfaces and prevents them from being fertilized so the trees will not bear fruit. The second method is to apply a hormone spray just after the tree is in full bloom but before the petals have dropped *(left)*. This arrests the growth of fruit.

For the best results, spray on cool, cloudy days and be sure you completely cover all flowers and leaves.

PRUNING THE EUROPEAN WAY

A pruning technique for deciduous trees that is popular in Europe can add a different look to an American garden. The technique, called pollarding, gives a stylized shape to the branches and limits the height of the tree.

Pollarding consists of cutting back all branches so that each spring, they produce a small, dense circle of foliage at their tips. Once a tree has reached about 8 feet in height, all the branches are cut back to between 2 to 4 feet in length. A round, thick crown will form at the end of each branch. In spring, short, slender branches will grow from the crown and produce clumps of foliage.

In fall, all of the new, thin branches are cut back to the crown. The cuts callus over, and each branch tip develops a knobby, circular growth that increases in size every year and gives the tree a distinctive silhouette.

PROTECTING TREES FROM WINTER DAMAGE

Sturdy and enduring though they seem, trees are as susceptible to winter damage as other plants in the garden. The foliage of broad-leaved evergreen trees loses water through evaporation, and if unable to replace the water from the frozen ground, the leaves can turn brown and drop off. The thin bark of trees such as birch and silver maple is prone to frost cracks, especially when the trees are young. And the limbs of needle-leaved evergreens can be broken or misshapen by the weight of accumulated snow and ice.

But you can take precautions against all these hazards. In late fall, water your broad-leaved evergreens well and spray them with an antidesiccant—a waxy liquid that coats the leaves and seals in moisture. Cover the trunks of your birches and silver maples with strips of burlap tied with string or with adhesive tree wrap (available at garden centers); wind it diagonally around each trunk *(left)*. If ice or snow remains on your pines and spruces after a storm, knock it off with a broom as soon as possible.

BEFORE YOU DIG . . .

Utility lines—gas mains, electric and telephone wires, television cables—may be anywhere in your yard. Some wires run overhead from curbside poles to rooftops; others lie buried underground. To strike any of them would risk not only a disruption of power and high costs for repairs, but injury to yourself and bystanders. For safety's sake, determine where they are. Many utility companies will send a surveyor to locate them for you.

When planting a tree, locate it where it will not grow into overhead wires. Existing trees may need watching, too. If any branches grow into the wires, do not prune them yourself; ask the appropriate utility company to send someone qualified to do the job safely.

AERATING ROOTS

To give a tree's roots a breath of fresh air, you can aerate the soil at the base of the trunk in spring. Aeration consists of making small holes in the soil so that more oxygen and water can get to the roots, most of which extend from the trunk to the drip line in the top 12 inches of soil. It is especially helpful for trees that are in the path of heavy foot traffic, which compresses the soil.

Aeration can be done with an ordinary pitchfork. There are also tools designed especially for the purpose; these are available at garden supply centers. The best tools lift plugs of soil out of the ground. Also available are automated aerating machines, which are useful if you have an orchard of large, established trees.

6
DICTIONARY OF TREES

Choosing trees is often the most important of all the decisions a gardener makes. Their size and longevity make them key elements in the framework of a garden, both from season to season and over many years. The right tree in the right place is an enduring pleasure, but a thoughtless selection can yield unwelcome surprises. One common mistake is not taking a tree's eventual height into account; another is neglecting to consider seasonal color. All too soon, a sapling can grow out of proportion to its surroundings, dwarfing a house or casting unwanted shade on sun-loving plants. And an attractive feature such as a tree's spring flowers can clash with the colors of a house or a nearby flower bed. Whether a tree is meant for beauty alone or to fill a practical function such as providing shade or privacy, a knowing choice will serve the gardener well.

With the dictionary that follows, you can familiarize yourself with a wide variety of trees, which are organized alphabetically by genera, or groups of closely related species. Each entry describes characteristics shared by the members of the genus and also points out the special traits of individual species, such as unusual foliage coloration or a limited hardiness range. A photograph illustrates each entry, and in some instances details of particular interest are highlighted with another, smaller photograph.

Since climate and soil have a major impact on a tree's growth, the ultimate sizes given here are approximate. For the same reasons, growth rates are also estimates. Trees designated as fast growers generally add more than 2 feet in height per year while they are young, slow growers less than a foot.

Each entry suggests appropriate ways to use trees in the landscape. Those recommended for streetside planting, for instance, have roots deep enough to leave sidewalks intact and do not drop messy fruits on parked cars. Those suggested for specimens, which stand alone in an expanse of lawn or ground cover, are attractive in more than one season, perhaps offering a sinuous silhouette in winter and broad, lush leaves in summer. You will also find many candidates for shade trees, as well as solutions for screening problems and for difficult spots such as seaside gardens.

ABIES CONCOLOR

ACACIA BAILEYANA

ACER GRISEUM

Abies (AY-beez)
Fir

Pyramidal evergreen that rises to heights of 30 to 150 feet. Branches are open and upright; needles are aromatic, flat, blunt-pointed and marked on the underside of most species by two whitish lines. Cones mature in a single season and grow upright, mostly near the top of the tree, on spreading branches. Zones 2-8.

Selected species and varieties
A. balsamea, balsam fir: grows 45 to 75 feet in height and 20 to 25 feet in spread, is lustrous-needled, fragrant and the most shade-tolerant of the firs. Balsam fir makes a good Christmas tree because it holds its needles. Zones 2-5. *A. concolor,* white fir: grows 30 to 50 feet in height and 15 to 30 feet in spread. Upward-curving needles are bluish or grayish green and 2 inches long. Zones 4-8. *A. firma,* Momi fir: Japanese species that grows up to 90 feet tall. Needles are leathery and dark green. Zones 6-8. *A. fraseri,* Fraser fir: grows 30 to 40 feet, occasionally more, in height, and 20 to 25 feet in spread. Leafy protrusions, called bracts, jut out conspicuously between the scales of the cones. Fraser fir makes a good Christmas tree because it holds its needles well. Zone 4. *A. homolepis,* Nikko fir: a silver fir that grows to nearly 65 feet in height. Has dense foliage and branchlets that are deeply grooved. Zones 5-7. *A. lasiocarpa arizonica,* Arizona corkbark fir: grows up to 100 feet tall. Has bluish foliage and thick, corky, white bark that turns grayish with age. Zones 5-7. *A. nordmanniana,* Nordmann fir: grows up to 80 feet tall, has luxurious dark green needles and 5- to 6-inch cones. Zones 5-7.

Growing conditions
Firs prefer full sun, but they will grow in partial shade. They require moist, well-drained, sandy, acid soil and should be sheltered from wind. Balsam fir does best in regions where mean summer temperatures are 70° F or less and rainfall is ample.

Landscape uses
Firs make good specimen trees, screens, accents and background plants on properties large enough to accommodate their massive size.

Acacia (a-KAY-sha)
Acacia, wattle

Broad-leaved evergreens that range from 5-foot shrubs to 90-foot trees. The trees have rounded crowns of feathery foliage, and clusters of fragrant yellow flowers that blossom in spring and are followed by dry pods. Zones 8-10.

Selected species and varieties
A. baileyana, Bailey's acacia, Cootamundra wattle: slender tree that grows 25 to 30 feet tall. Has billows of small, bright, golden cotton-ball-like flowers that cluster over ferny, grayish blue foliage from January to March. Zone 10. *A. farnesiana,* sweet acacia: shrubby tree that grows up to 10 feet tall. Has thorny branches, flower clusters that blossom in February and March, and leaves composed of tiny leaflets less than ½ inch long. Zones 8 and 9. *A. longifolia,* Sydney golden wattle: small, vigorous tree that grows 25 feet in height and in spread; has flower heads in loose 2¼-inch-long spikes and willowy blue-green leaves. *A. melanoxylon,* blackwood: grows to 40 feet or more with cream-colored flowers on short spikes. Fruit is a twisted, dry pod. Zone 8.

Growing conditions
Acacia is fast growing, 4 feet or more per year. It requires full sun and moist soil, and a warm, dry climate. Bailey's acacia is drought-tolerant once established. Sydney golden wattle withstands salt spray. Cool summer nights and relatively dry winters produce quality blooms on both species. Prune trees after they have flowered.

Landscape uses
Acacia is a good street tree or accent plant in frost-free climates. In cold climates it should be container-grown to protect its tender roots from freezing.

Acer (AY-ser)
Maple

Deciduous trees 15 to 75 feet tall. All have dense, round crowns and colorful fall leaves that are palmately lobed and long-stalked. In most species, nonshowy flowers appear in early spring before leaves emerge. Fruits are paired winged seeds called samaras, or keys; they mature either in spring or in fall. Zones 2-9.

Selected species and varieties

A. buergeranum, trident maple: bushy, small tree that grows 15 to 30 feet. It has flaking orange-brown bark and 3-inch, pointed, shiny trilobed leaves, which are glossy dark green in summer and yellow, orange and red in fall. Greenish yellow flowers appear in May. Zones 6-8. *A. campestre,* hedge maple: reaches 35 feet or more. Leaves have three to five rounded lobes, stems are corky, and greenish flower heads appear in early spring. Zones 5-8. *A. ginnala,* Amur maple: grows 15 to 20 feet tall. Fragrant flowers are pale yellow. Leaves are simple, toothed and trilobed, with the largest lobe in the center; they are glossy green in spring and summer, and turn red or orange in fall. Winged seeds are red in fall. Zones 2-6. *A. griseum,* paperbark maple: so called because its cinnamon to red-brown bark peels in papery strips. Grows 20 to 30 feet or more in height with an open branching habit. Leaves are composed of three coarsely toothed leaflets; they often turn scarlet in fall. Zones 5-7.

A. japonicum 'Aconitifolium', fern-leaf full moon maple: rounded tree that grows to 10 to 15 feet with finely textured leaves. It flowers in mid-April and turns crimson in fall. Zones 5-8. 'Aureum' grows up to 20 feet in height and width and has pale golden yellow leaves. *A. negundo,* box elder, ash-leaved maple: grows 30 to 50 feet in height and spread. Has a rounded crown and irregular branches. Leaves are ovate to oblong, 2 to 4 inches long, and turn yellow-green to brown in autumn. Gray-brown bark is slightly furrowed. 'Variegatum' has leaves edged in white. Zones 5-8. *A. palmatum,* Japanese maple: grows 15 to 20 feet tall. Leaves are saw-toothed and turn brilliant yellow, bronze or purplish in fall. Zones 6-8. 'Atropurpureum': slow growing and hardier than most other cultivars. Zones 5-8. 'Bloodgood': graceful, compact cultivar, with foliage that is bright red when it emerges and darkens as the season progresses. The tree holds its color better than other red-leaf cultivars. 'Senkaki' has leaves that are bronze in spring, green in summer and red in fall. Its coral red bark is attractive in a winter landscape. *A. plat-*

anoides, Norway maple: grows to 50 feet with large, five-lobed, leathery leaves that are broader than they are long and sometimes turn yellow in fall. Greenish yellow flower clusters appear in spring. Winged paired fruit are shaped like coat hangers. Bark is dark and uniformly fissured. Zones 3-7. 'Columnare' has leaves that are smaller than those of the species; it is columnar in shape, with branches that spread at a 30° to 60° angle from a central trunk. 'Crimson King' has deep red leaves.

A. pseudoplatanus, sycamore maple: grows 40 to 60 feet tall and has light gray bark that peels to expose orange-brown inner bark. Zones 5-7. *A. rubrum,* red maple: grows 40 to 50 feet and is one of the first trees to flower in spring. Leaves are usually trilobed, toothed, whitish underneath and turn red in fall. Bark is light gray on young trees; becomes dark gray with vertical, platelike ridges as the tree ages. The tree has red flowers in spring and red winged pods in fall. Zones 3-9. 'October Glory' has shiny leaves that turn brilliant orange to red in autumn but fade before they drop from the tree. 'Red Sunset' has bright green leaves that turn orange or scarlet in early fall.

A. saccharinum, silver maple: a large, spreading tree that grows 50 to 70 feet tall and 35 to 45 feet across. It has long, pendulous branches; deeply cut, pointed five-lobed leaves; and twigs that emit an unpleasant odor when bruised. Bark exfoliates to show orange undertones. Suckers emerge at the base of the trunk. Silver maple has little, if any, fall color. It is short-lived, but hardy and aggressive and a good tree for poor soils where hardly anything else will grow. Zones 3-9. *A. saccharum,* sugar maple: a relatively short-trunked tree with a large crown that gives it a total of 60 to 75 feet in height and a 40- to 50-foot spread. Leaves are three- to five-lobed, as broad as they are long, and turn yellow, burnt orange and tones of red in autumn. Chartreuse flowers emerge in April, and fruit is produced in fall. Zones 3-8. 'Bonfire' is a heat-tolerant, vigorous maple with leaves that turn carmine red in fall. 'Fairview' has lighter colored bark than other maples and leaves that turn yellow in fall. *A. tataricum,* tatarian maple: grows

ACER JAPONICUM 'AUREUM'

ACER RUBRUM

ACER SACCHARUM

AESCULUS × CARNEA 'BRIOTII'

AESCULUS HIPPOCASTANUM

AILANTHUS ALTISSIMA

20 to 30 feet tall and just as wide. Leaves are 2 to 4 inches wide, toothed, dark green in summer and turn yellow to red in fall. Zones 4-7.

Growing conditions
All maples can grow in full sun or partial shade except for Japanese maple, which grows only in partial shade. Most need moist, well-drained soil. Trident maple tolerates a variety of soil conditions —wetness, salt and compaction. Hedge maple adapts to alkaline soil. Amur maple tolerates drought and cold. Paperbark will grow in clay, and it should be pruned in summer for its attractive branching habit to show. Red maple and silver maple may split in winter storms. Sugar maple cannot tolerate road salt. Tatarian tolerates drought.

Landscape uses
Trident maple makes a good medium-size patio plant, street tree or specimen. Hedge maple is best used as a screen or hedge. Amur maple is a good specimen tree; it is also small enough to be container-grown and makes a good bonsai subject. The bright-colored peeling bark and the open branching of paperbark maple make it an attractive specimen tree all year round. Japanese maple and fern-leaf full moon maple, because they are diminutive in size, make good accents in patio gardens and courtyards. Norway maple tolerates urban pollution better than most maples and is therefore useful as a street tree. Grass is difficult to grow underneath Norway, red and sugar maples because of their shallow surface roots. Silver maple grows so fast it provides quick shade, but it should not be used as a street tree because its limbs break easily in winter storms, and its roots push up sidewalks and buckle drain tiles. Sugar maple is a good shade tree.

—

Aesculus (ES-kew-lus)
Horse chestnut, buckeye

Deciduous flowering tree that grows 20 to 50 feet tall. It has compound leaves shaped like the spokes of a wheel, and glossy brown husked nuts. Zones 4-8.

Selected species and varieties
A. × carnea 'Briotii': a cultivar that grows 25 to 40 feet, has large, ruby red flower heads and pointed palmate leaves that are dark, glossy green. It is pyramidal as a young tree but becomes roundheaded when mature. Zones 5-8. *A. glabra,* Ohio buckeye: grows up to 40 feet tall and has a low-branching habit. Small yellow-green flowers occur in erect, 6-inch clusters. Zones 5-8. *A. hippocastanum,* European horse chestnut: grows to 40 feet and has upright clusters of white flowers in May. It bears elliptical leaflets that are 4 to 10 inches long, and it produces shiny brown seeds in large, spiny husks. Zones 5-8. *A. octandra,* sometimes designated *A. flava,* yellow buckeye, sweet buckeye: grows up to 70 feet tall in an oval, upright form with spreading branches. Fruit is 2 to 2½ inches long and pear-shaped. Bark is mottled gray and brown. Zones 5-8. *A. pavia,* pavia, red buckeye: small tree that reaches 20 feet. It produces loose clusters of red flowers in June. Zones 6-8.

Growing conditions
Horse chestnut needs full sun and deep, moist, fertile soil.

Landscape uses
Horse chestnuts are good shade trees for wide, open spaces. They are not for small city lots or sidewalks because their flowers and fruit produce litter.

—

Ailanthus (Ay-LAN-thus)
Tree-of-heaven

Fast-growing deciduous tree that reaches 60 feet or more and can spread to two-thirds of its height. It has very large, dark green leaves that are ill-scented when bruised, and winged seeds. Zones 4-9.

Selected species and varieties
A. altissima: has 18- to 24-inch-long compound leaves composed of oval-shaped leaflets, which vary greatly in number. Flowers are small, yellow clusters that bloom in summer. Winged seeds are yellow-green to orange-red in summer, changing to brown and persisting in winter.

Growing conditions
Tree-of-heaven grows in full sun and partial shade, and it adapts to any kind of soil.

Landscape uses
Tree-of-heaven is suited for impossible conditions where no other

tree will survive; it withstands urban pollution, highway salting and poor soil. If you use it, plant a seed-bearing female; male flowers produce a vile odor.

—

Albizia (al-BIZZ-ee-a)

Deciduous flowering tree that grows from 20 to 120 feet tall or more. It is flat-topped, wide-spreading and low-branched. It blooms in midsummer, has feathery, fernlike foliage that folds inward when touched and produces long, beanlike seedpods in autumn. Zones 6-10.

Selected species and varieties
A. julibrissin, silk tree, mimosa: grows to 40 feet with 9- to 12-inch-long leaves and pink flowers. Zones 7-9. The cultivars 'Charlotte' and 'Tryon' have rosy pink, powder-puff-like flowers and are resistant to mimosa wilt disease. 'Rosea' has deeper pink blossoms and is hardier than 'Charlotte' or 'Tryon'. Zones 6-9.

Growing conditions
Silk tree does best in full sun and well-drained soil. It tolerates dry, hot summers and polluted areas.

Landscape uses
Albizia makes a good shade tree, ornamental or accent plant.

—

Alder see *Alnus*

—

Alnus (AL-nus)
Alder

Deciduous tree that grows 40 to 70 feet tall. It has flowers that emerge from catkins in spring and are followed by toothed leaves and cone-like fruits. Zones 2-7.

Selected species and varieties
A. cordata, Italian alder: grows 30 to 50 feet tall in a pyramidal to rounded form. Leaves are ovate and 2 to 4 inches long. Zones 5-7. *A. glutinosa*, common alder, black alder: grows up to 60 feet tall and sometimes develops an oval or oblong crown. Flowers are red or purple. Bark is glossy and dark brown. Zones 3-7. 'Imperialis' has deeply cut leaves. 'Pyramidalis' grows to 50 feet; it is narrow, upright, dense and low-branched.

A. incana, white alder: grows 40 to 60 feet tall. It has dull, dark green foliage.

Growing conditions
Alder grows in full sun or partial shade. It does best in wet or moist soil but tolerates dry soil.

Landscape uses
In mass plantings, alders make good screens.

—

Alsophila see *Sphaeropteris*

—

Amelanchier (am-el-ANK-ee-er)
Serviceberry, Juneberry, shadbush

Small deciduous flowering tree that grows 20 to 30 feet tall in a rounded shape. Has snowy white 1-inch flowers that are among the first to bloom in spring and are followed in summer by sweet red or purple berry-like fruit. Leaves turn yellow, orange or red in fall. Smooth gray bark is streaked with reddish longitudinal fissures. Zones 3-8.

Selected species and varieties
A. arborea, downy serviceberry: pointed, finely toothed leaves are grayish green in spring and turn a deeper green in summer. *A. × grandiflora*, apple serviceberry: a naturally occurring hybrid between downy serviceberry and Allegheny serviceberry with larger flowers than either. Zones 4-8. *A. laevis*, Allegheny serviceberry: leaves are purplish when they emerge and later turn dark green. Fruit is purple to black. Zones 4-8.

Growing conditions
Serviceberry tolerates either full sun or partial shade. It prefers moist soil but can adapt to a wide variety of soils. It seldom needs fertilizing and needs pruning only to control suckers.

Landscape uses
Serviceberry lends itself to naturalizing at the edge of a wood. As a specimen tree it has four-season interest with its colorful flowers, fruit, leaves and bark.

—

Aralia (a-RAIL-ee-a)

Deciduous tree that grows up to 50 feet tall with a nearly equal spread.

ALBIZIA JULIBRISSIN 'ROSEA'

ALNUS CORDATA

AMELANCHIER LAEVIS

ARALIA ELATA

101

ARAUCARIA ARAUCANA

ARBUTUS UNEDO

BAUHINIA FORFICATA

It tends to be shrubby and is armed with spiny twigs. Flowers are white or greenish; fruit is usually black. Zones 2-9.

Selected species and varieties
A. elata, Japanese angelica: grows 30 to 50 feet in an umbrella-like shape. Leaves are 3 feet long, with many 2- to 5-inch prickly leaflets. Small white flowers in large clusters open in August and are followed in autumn by abundant dark fruit. Zones 4-9.

Growing conditions
Japanese angelica tolerates full sun or partial shade. It prefers well-drained moist soil but will adapt to dry, rocky or heavy soil.

Landscape uses
Japanese angelica's shrubby form and prickly twigs make it useful as a privacy thicket. To maintain an umbrella shape and use it for a specimen tree, prune its suckers regularly.

—

Araucaria (A-rah-KAY-ree-a)

Tall, pyramid-shaped evergreen conifer that grows 70 feet or more. The trunk often sheds its lower branches as the tree ages. Zones 8-10.

Selected species and varieties
A. araucana, monkey puzzle: grows to 90 feet. Has ascending, twisted, ropelike branches; sharp, green, scalelike needles and gray, ringed bark. Zones 8-9. *A. bidwilli,* bunya bunya: narrow, pyramidal tree that grows to 80 feet. Needles are glossy. Zone 10. *A. heterophylla,* Norfolk Island pine: subtropical species that grows to 70 feet or more. Has soft, bright green needles. Zone 10.

Growing conditions
Araucarias prefer sun except for Norfolk Island pine, which prefers partial shade. Monkey puzzle does best in moist soil, bunya bunya tolerates desert conditions, and Norfolk Island pine adapts to a variety of conditions.

Landscape uses
Alone, araucarias make good specimen trees; in mass plantings they make good windbreaks. But beware of falling cones, which are heavy and hazardous. In cool climates, Norfolk Island pine can be container-grown outdoors in warm

weather and brought indoors for the winter.

—

Arborvitae see *Thuja*

—

Arbutus (ar-BEW-tus)
Manzanita

Ornamental broad-leaved evergreen that grows 20 to 100 feet tall. Flowers are white or pale pink, fruits are berry-like and rounded, and foliage is glossy. Zones 7 and 8.

Selected species and varieties
A. menziesii, madrone: grows up to 75 feet tall. Has small, white, 9-inch-long flower clusters in May and red-orange berries in fall. Older bark peels back to reveal lighter cinnamon bark underneath. Zone 7. *A. unedo,* strawberry tree: slow growing to 20 to 30 feet. Has serrated leaves, drooping flower clusters of white or pink from October to December, and edible but tasteless fruit that looks something like strawberries. 'Compacta' has deep green foliage tinted with amber and abundant white flowers in fall. 'Elfin King' is a dwarf and has a reddish cast to its new growth. Zone 8.

Growing conditions
Arbutus needs sun and protection from wind. It prefers dry, sandy and acid soil.

Landscape uses
Arbutus is a good specimen or accent plant, but its shedding bark, flowers and fruit can cause litter.

—

Ash see *Fraxinus*

Aspen see *Populus*

Australian pine see *Casuarina*

Balsam fir see *Abies*

Basswood see *Tilia*

—

Bauhinia (baw-HIN-ee-a)

Broad-leaved evergreen that grows slowly to 6 to 40 feet. Flowers are 6 inches across and resemble orchids. Leaves are two-lobed and resemble cloven hooves. Zones 9 and 10.

Selected species and varieties
B. blakeana, Hong Kong orchid

tree: 40-foot tree with fragrant, reddish to rose purple flowers that bloom from winter to spring. *B. forficata:* grows to 30 feet and has drooping branches lined with ¼-inch spines. Flowers are white, up to 5 inches across and shaped like butterflies; they are followed in fall by flat ⅛-inch pods. *B. purpurea,* butterfly tree, purple orchid tree: grows 25 to 30 feet tall with rounded crown and fragrant purplish flowers. *B. variegata,* orchid tree, mountain ebony: grows 20 to 40 feet tall with magenta, purple or white flowers. 'Candida', orchid tree: has white flowers with a hint of light green.

Growing conditions
Bauhinia prefers full sun but will tolerate partial shade. It does best in moist, well-drained soil, and in warm, dry climates.

Landscape uses
Bauhinia makes a very good specimen or accent tree because of its showy blossoms.

—

Bay laurel see *Laurus*

Beech see *Fagus*

Beefwood see *Casuarina*

—

Betula (BET-yew-la)
Birch

Deciduous tree that grows 40 to 100 feet tall. Has slender branches, flowers borne in catkins and double-toothed leaves that turn yellow in autumn. Bark varies in color from white, silver, yellow-orange, reddish brown to near black. Zones 4-9.

Selected species and varieties
B. albosinensis septentrionalis, Chinese paper birch: grows 40 to 60 feet tall and has curling red-orange bark. Zones 5-7. *B. alleghaniensis,* yellow birch: grows 60 to 70 feet tall. Leaves are dull, dark green on upper surfaces and pale yellow-green on the undersides in summer, and change to yellow in fall. Bark on young trees is yellow or bronze and shreds; on older trees it is reddish brown and peels off in large plates. Zones 3-5. *B. maximowicziana,* monarch birch: grows 45 to 50 feet tall. Leaves are heart-shaped and bark is orange-gray. Zones 5 and 6. *B.*

nigra, river birch: reaches 100 feet in height. Bark is shaggy and tannish with pink and orange undertones. 'Heritage' has salmon white, peeling bark. Zones 4-9. *B. papyrifera,* paper birch, canoe birch, white birch: reaches 50 feet or more, may be multi- or single-stemmed, and has striking white bark. Zones 2-5. *B. pendula,* European white birch: grows 40 to 50 feet tall. The crown is pyramidal in youth and becomes oval as the tree matures. Bark flakes off in layers. Leaves are toothed and up to ¾ inch long. Zones 2-6. 'Dalecarlica', silver birch: has particularly pendulous branches and leaves that are deeply lobed to within ⅛ inch of the midrib. 'Purpurea', purple-leaf European birch: grows to 50 feet. Young leaves emerge deep purple in spring and fade in summer. Zones 3-5. *B. platyphylla japonica* 'Whitespire', whitespire birch: grows 40 to 50 feet in a pyramidal shape. Zones 4-7.

Growing conditions
Most birches grow in full sun. They prefer moist, cool soil but can tolerate poor soil in the North. Canoe birch should be planted on a slope that faces north. Monarch birch tolerates urban pollution. River birch should not be planted in alkaline soil.

Landscape uses
Birch is a good shade tree. It can be naturalized in a woodsy border.

—

Birch see *Betula*

Box elder see *Acer*

Buckeye see *Aesculus*

Buddhist pine see *Podocarpus*

Bunya bunya see *Araucaria*

Butterfly tree see *Bauhinia*

Butternut see *Juglans*

Buttonwood see *Platanus*

Cabbage palm see *Sabal*

California incense cedar
see *Calocedrus*

—

Calocedrus (kal-o-SEE-drus)

Stately, columnar, needle-leaved evergreen that grows 30 to 100 feet tall. It has tiny, scalelike green foliage and flattened stems. Zones 6-9.

BETULA PAPYRIFERA

CALOCEDRUS DECURRENS

CARPINUS BETULUS

CARPINUS JAPONICA

CARYA OVATA

CASSIA EXCELSA

Selected species and varieties

C. decurrens, California incense cedar: aromatic tree that grows 50 feet or more. Lower branches grow close to the ground. Needles retain their shiny green color year round. Bark is reddish brown and peels. Cones appear in autumn and persist until spring.

Growing conditions

California incense cedar must have full sun, humid atmosphere and moist soil. It cannot tolerate smog or wind.

Landscape uses

The columnar form of calocedrus makes the tree suitable for formal plantings in large areas. It may be used singly as a specimen, or in massed planting as a screen.

—

Carpinus (kar-PY-nus)
Hornbeam

Deciduous tree that grows slowly to heights ranging from 20 to 60 feet. It has toothed, prominently ribbed leaves, spring-flowering catkins and nutlets in leafy bracts that ripen in autumn. Trunks are short and covered with fluted gray bark. Zones 3-9.

Selected species and varieties

C. betulus, European hornbeam: grows to 40 to 60 feet in height and 30 to 40 feet in width. The tree is rounded in shape and has dark green leaves that sometimes turn yellow. Zones 5-7. 'Columnaris' is slow growing, narrow, steeple-shaped and has dense foliage. 'Fastigiata' becomes oval to vase-shaped with age and has dense, ascending branches. *C. caroliniana,* American hornbeam, blue beech, ironwood, muscle-wood, water beech: a small tree that grows to 35 feet with an irregular branching habit and dark bluish gray bark. In autumn, leaves become red-orange and bracts containing nutlets turn brown. Zones 4-7. *C. japonica,* Japanese hornbeam: a small 20- to 30-foot tree with branches that spread to form a fanlike crown. Zones 5-7.

Growing conditions

Hornbeam grows in sun or shade and in any moist, well-drained soil.

Landscape uses

Hornbeam makes a good street tree, shade tree or specimen. Sev-

eral together in a massed planting make a good windbreak. European hornbeam takes heavy shearing as a hedge. American and Japanese hornbeams are useful as patio trees, and because of their size they can grow as understory plants—small trees under the cover of taller trees.

—

Carya (KAY-ree-a)
Hickory

Deciduous nut tree that grows 60 to 100 feet tall. Has a husk-encased, hard-shelled, bony nut that drops in October; the nut may be either tasty or bitter, depending on species. Pendulous catkins emerge in April or May along with the leaves. Zones 4-9.

Selected species and varieties

C. illinoinensis, pecan: grows 70 to 100 feet in height and 40 to 75 feet in width. Thin, aromatic husks enclose reddish brown edible nuts. Compound leaves, 9 to 20 inches long, are composed of nine to 17 sickle-shaped leaflets. They are aromatic when crushed. Zones 5-9; *C. laciniosa,* shellbark hickory: grows 60 to 80 feet tall with a narrow crown and short, stout limbs. Leaves generally bear five to nine leaflets and turn golden brown in fall. Zones 5-8. *C. ovata,* shagbark hickory: grows to 100 feet with an oblong crown. Has gray, shaggy bark that peels in vertical plates and golden autumn foliage. Zones 4-9.

Growing conditions

Pecan and hickory trees need full sun and fertile, deep, moist, well-drained soil.

Landscape uses

Hickory makes a majestic specimen tree on a spacious lawn.

—

Cassia (KASS-ee-a)
Senna, shower tree

Showy flowering tropical tree that grows up to 40 feet in height. Zones 9 and 10.

Selected species and varieties

C. excelsa: grows up to 30 feet tall. Has brilliant yellow flowers in summer. Leaves have 10 to 20 pairs of leaflets. Zone 10. *C. fistula,* golden shower tree: grows to 30 feet. Has fragrant, 2-inch yellow flowers that cascade in 1- to 1½-foot sprays;

they bloom from spring through summer. Dark seedpods are 1 foot or more in length. Leaves have four to six pairs of leaflets and remain on the trees late into winter.

Growing conditions
Shower trees will grow in full sun or partial shade and in any well-drained soil.

Landscape uses
Shower tree is an ornamental accent plant.

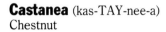

Castanea (kas-TAY-nee-a)
Chestnut

Massive deciduous nut-producing tree that grows 40 to 100 feet tall. Leaves are long, narrow and coarsely toothed. Flowering catkins emerge in summer after the leaves. Spiny husks enclose two or three shiny brown nuts that ripen in autumn. Zones 4-8.

Selected species and varieties
C. mollissima, Chinese chestnut: grows 40 to 60 feet in height, with a dense, rounded crown. Leaves are red when unfolding, become a rich, leathery, dark green in summer and turn bronzy yellow in late autumn. Flowers are cream-colored. Bark is grayish brown and furrowed.

Growing conditions
Chinese chestnut needs full sun, sandy, acid soil and plenty of fertilizer. It is drought-resistant.

Landscape uses
Chinese chestnut has replaced the blighted American chestnut as a specimen tree.

Casuarina (kas-ew-a-REE-na)
Australian pine

Tall, fast-growing evergreen that reaches 70 feet. It has long, slender branches and wiry, jointed branchlets with needle-like leaves occurring in whorls. Zones 9 and 10.

Selected species and varieties
C. cunninghamiana, Australian pine, beefwood, she-oak: tree with upward-spreading branches. *C. equisetifolia,* horsetail tree: low-branching tree with branchlets that are approximately 1/32 inch in diameter. Fruit is 1/2 inch long and cone-shaped.

Growing conditions
Australian pines do best in full sun and brackish soil.

Landscape uses
Australian pines hold soil well and are therefore useful at the seashore. They make good wind-breaks, hedges, street trees and specimens.

Catalpa (ka-TAL-pa)

Deciduous shade tree that grows 30 to 90 feet tall. It has opposite, sometimes whorled, leaves that are heart-shaped and are downy on the underside, conspicuous summer flowers and long, beanlike seed capsules known as Indian cigars that hang on throughout the winter. Zones 4-9.

Selected species and varieties
C. bignonioides, southern catalpa: ornamental tree of broad, spreading growth, with stout, brittle branches, 30 to 40 feet tall. Leaves are 4 to 8 inches long, unfurl in late June and turn black before falling. Flowers are white, spotted with yellow and purple, and emerge in midsummer. Foot-long seedpods decorate the tree in fall. Bark has loose, thin scales. Zones 5-9. *C. speciosa,* northern catalpa: grows 50 to 80 feet. It has an upright, irregular silhouette and conspicuous twigs, especially in winter. Stems are knobby. Masses of early-summer blooms are followed by hard, long seedpods. Gray-brown bark has coarse, elongated ridges and furrows.

Growing conditions
Catalpa likes sun and thrives in hot, dry summers. It is a tough tree and adapts to a wide variety of soil types.

Landscape uses
Catalpa makes a good shade tree on a lawn that is large enough to accommodate it.

Cedar see *Cedrus*

Cedrus (SEE-drus)
Cedar

Needle-leaved evergreen that grows 40 to 60 feet or more. It has graceful, wide-spreading branches and fragrant wood. Zones 5-9.

CASTANEA MOLLISSIMA

CASUARINA EQUISETIFOLIA

CATALPA BIGNONIOIDES

CEDRUS ATLANTICA 'GLAUCA'

CELTIS LAEVIGATA

CERCIDIPHYLLUM JAPONICUM

CERCIS CANADENSIS 'ALBA'

CERCIS CANADENSIS 'FOREST PANSY'

Selected species and varieties

C. atlantica 'Glauca', blue atlas cedar: grows to 60 feet. It is conical in youth, becoming flat-topped as it matures. Its needles are smooth and silvery blue. Zones 6-9. *C. deodara*, deodar cedar: reaches 50 feet in height. Has graceful horizontal branches that droop at their tips. Its needles are soft and green. Zones 7-9. *C. libani*, cedar of Lebanon: has a shorter crown than atlas cedar. It is the hardiest of the true cedars. Zones 5-8.

Growing conditions

Deodar cedar and cedar of Lebanon need sun and like dry soil; atlas cedar is adaptable and can take sun or partial shade. Any good garden soil will support them all.

Landscape uses

Singly, cedars make outstanding specimen trees. Their branches are spread so wide that three together can make an effective screen. Blue atlas cedar is used as an accent plant when silvery blue is wanted for landscape design.

Celtis (SELL-tis)
Hackberry

Deciduous tree that grows 70 to 80 feet in height with a rounded crown. Leaves are ovate and generally toothed. Fruit is fleshy, berry-like and orange-red to blue-black. Zones 4-9.

Selected species and varieties

C. laevigata, sugar hackberry: has a crown that spreads up to 80 feet in width. Zones 6-9. *C. occidentalis*, common hackberry: has a tall, oval crown, bark that is gray and vertically ridged, and leaves that turn yellow in fall. Zones 4-8.

Growing conditions

Hackberries require full sun. They prefer moist soil, but they will grow in dry, heavy, sandy and rocky soils and tolerate wind and urban pollution.

Landscape uses

Hackberries make good shade trees; they grow rapidly and thus can provide shade in a few years' time. They also make good street trees because of their resistance to pollution and because their roots grow so deep that they do not crack sidewalks.

Cercidiphyllum
(ser-sid-i-FILL-lum)

Deciduous ornamental that is oval-shaped and grows to 40 feet in 20 years. May be single- or multiple-trunked, with slender ascending branches that spread when mature. Zones 5-9.

Selected species and varieties

C. japonicum, Katsura tree: grows 40 to 60 feet or more with airy, open form. It has fine-textured foliage that is purplish bronze when unfolding, turns bluish green in summer and changes to yellow or apricot in fall. Stems are slender and have red tips throughout the summer. Floral bracts open before the leaves in March or April. Bark is shaggy and grayish brown. Small seedpods appear in October and are persistent. Zones 4-9.

Growing conditions

Katsura tree needs full sun and moist, well-drained soil. Where climate is hot and dry it should have protection from summer sun.

Landscape uses

Katsura tree gives dappled shade in summer, and its shaggy bark offers interest all year round.

Cercis (SER-sis)
Redbud

Graceful, 20- to 40-foot deciduous tree having branches that arch horizontally. After a shower of small flowers in spring, lush, heart-shaped foliage appears. Zones 5-9.

Selected species and varieties

C. canadensis, eastern redbud: grows 20 to 30 feet with a 30-foot spread. Has magenta pink flowers on zigzagging branchlets. Fruits are in small, papery seedpods. Falling leaves exude a pleasant, spicy scent. Zones 5-8. 'Alba' has white flowers. 'Forest Pansy' has leaves that emerge reddish purple and turn dark green in summer. Flowers are darker than the standard magenta pink. 'Wither's Pink Charm' has soft pink blossoms, paler than those of the species, and is hardier than 'Alba'. *C. reniformis*, Texas redbud: has rounded, leathery foliage and is less cold-hardy than eastern redbud. Zones 8 and 9.

Growing conditions

Redbud grows in full sun and partial shade and in any well-drained soil.

Landscape uses
Redbud makes a good lawn accent or specimen tree. It is also effective naturalized in a woodland border.

—

Chamaecyparis
(kam-ee-SIP-a-ris)
False cypress

Pyramidal evergreen conifer that grows 40 to 100 feet. It has flat sprays of scalelike leaves marked with white on the undersides. Reddish brown bark shreds. Zones 5-9.

Selected species and varieties
C. lawsoniana, Lawson false cypress: reaches 50 feet. Soft leaves vary from bright green to blue-green to yellow, depending on the cultivar. Zones 6 and 7. *C. nootkatensis,* Nootka false cypress: dense evergreen that grows to 100 feet or more. It lacks the white underside markings typical of most species; leaf sprays are rough to the touch and emit a pungent odor when bruised. Cones are pointed. 'Pendula' is fast growing, with graceful, drooping branchlets and soft, blue-green foliage, without the white markings typical of most false cypresses. It can live for hundreds of years under the right climatic conditions. *C. pisifera,* sawara false cypress: grows up to 70 feet. Leaves can be feathery or mosslike; colors range from bright green to dark green to bluish green. Zones 5-8. 'Golden Thread' grows to 10 feet tall and has weeping, golden threadlike foliage. *C. thyoides,* Atlantic white cedar, swamp cedar: has a narrow, conical head and grows 40 to 60 feet. *C. thyoides* 'Hopkinton': a columnar tree that grows rapidly to 60 feet. It has aromatic, blue-gray foliage and bears many small cones in winter.

Growing conditions
False cypress needs sun, but cool temperatures, high humidity and protection from wind. Soil should be moist and well drained.

Landscape uses
Tall species of false cypress provide vertical accents as specimen trees. Medium-tall species make good screens. Short species are useful as foundation plants.

—

Cherry see *Prunus*

Chestnut see *Castanea*

China fir see *Cunninghamia*

Chinese flame tree see *Koelreuteria*

Chinese fountain plant see *Livistona*

Chinese parasol tree see *Firmiana*

Chinese scholar tree see *Sophora*

Chinese tallow tree see *Sapium*

—

Chorisia (kor-IS-ee-a)
Floss silk tree

Tropical ornamental tree that grows to 50 feet, having big, exotic blooms and silky seed floss used for making pillow stuffing. Trunk is oddly bottle-shaped and prickly. Zones 9 and 10.

Selected species and varieties
C. speciosa: has 3- to 5-inch reddish white flowers in fall, followed by pear-shaped, floss-bearing pods. Zone 10.

Growing conditions
Floss silk tree needs full sun. It likes heat and fertile soil.

Landscape uses
Floss silk tree is a good specimen or street tree.

—

Cladrastis (klad-RAS-tis)
Yellowwood

Deciduous flowering ornamental tree that grows 20 to 50 feet or more. It has a graceful, rounded crown and fragrant blossoms that cascade from slender, zigzagging branches in late May and early June. Zones 4-8.

Selected species and varieties
C. lutea: leaves are composed of seven to nine leaflets; they emerge yellowish green, turn bright green in summer and yellow in autumn. Flowers are white; thin, flat, drooping seedpods follow in autumn. The bark is smooth and gray. Zones 4-8.

Growing conditions
Yellowwood needs full sun and is drought-resistant once it is established. It thrives in almost any well-drained soil. It needs a few years after transplanting before it flowers, and then the flowering is

CHAMAECYPARIS NOOTKATENSIS

CHAMAECYPARIS PISIFERA 'GOLDEN THREAD'

CHORISIA SPECIOSA

CLADRASTIS LUTEA

COCOS NUCIFERA

CORNUS FLORIDA 'RUBRA'

CORNUS FLORIDA 'WELCHII'

CORYLUS COLURNA

best every other year or two. Prune yellowwood only in summer to avoid sap bleeding.

Landscape uses
Yellowwood's combination of springtime flowers and crooked branches make it an attractive specimen tree all year round, and in summer it provides good shade. But it lures bumblebees; beware of planting it where children play.

Coconut palm see *Cocos*

Cocos (KO-kos)
Coconut palm

Fountain-shaped tropical tree that grows 100 to 130 feet. It has long, graceful leaves and large edible fruits encased in tough husks composed of strong tan fiber. Zones 8-10.

Selected species and varieties
C. nucifera: trunk is capped with a magnificent crown of leathery, 12- to 18-foot swaying branches. Leaves are glossy and evergreen. Trees fruit after about five years of age and produce clusters of coconuts in great numbers thereafter.

Growing conditions
Coconut palm grows in full sun and in sandy soil that is rich in organic matter. It needs practically no care except that dead branches should be pruned and removed promptly to avoid an unkempt, ragged look.

Landscape uses
Coconut palm makes a good street tree and specimen in warm seashore areas.

Coral tree see *Erythrina*
Cork tree see *Phellodendron*

Cornus (KOR-nus)
Dogwood

Deciduous ornamental trees that grow from 15 to 40 feet and are generally wider than they are tall. They have year-round interest: flowers in spring, fruit in summer, wine-colored foliage in autumn and a picturesque silhouette in winter. Zones 3-8.

Selected species and varieties
C. alternifolia, pagoda dogwood: open-branched tree that grows 15 to 25 feet. Leaves tend to be concentrated near the ends of the branches. Abundant, flat-topped flower clusters appear in May with bluish black fruit following in July or August. Zones 3-7. *C. florida,* flowering dogwood: reaches 15 to 40 feet. Minuscule yellow true flowers are surrounded by white, sometimes pink, showy bracts that open in spring. Clustered red fruits follow, and leaves turn scarlet in fall. Bark is blocky and coarse. Zones 6-9. 'Cherokee Chief' has deep rosy red bracts instead of white ones. Zones 6-8. 'Cherokee Princess' has large, early- and abundantly flowering bracts. Zones 6-8. 'Cloud Nine' has abundant, showy white bracts. 'Junior Miss' has large bracts that are deep pink shading to white in the center. 'Rubra' blooms later than most cultivars and does not flower consistently. 'Welchii' has variegated creamy white, pink and green leaves. *C. kousa,* Kousa dogwood: has pointed, white flower-like bracts that appear in June, later than flowering dogwood, and turn pink with age. Red, raspberry-like, dangling fruit follows from August to October. *C. kousa chinensis:* includes Chinese cultivars, such as 'Milky Way', which flowers heavily, and 'Summer Stars', which has bracts that hang on for about six weeks. Zones 5-8.

Growing conditions
Dogwoods need partial shade and cool, acid, well-drained soil.

Landscape uses
Dogwoods make spectacular specimens and accents—in spring for their showy flowers, in summer for their fruits, and some species in winter for their colorful bark. They are small enough to use on patios; and because they do best in partial shade, they thrive as understory plants—small trees under the cover of taller ones.

Corylus (KOR-il-us)
Filbert, hazelnut

Group of deciduous nut trees that are related to the birch family and grow from 25 to 120 feet tall. Zones 4-8.

Selected species and varieties
C. colurna, Turkish filbert: a pyramidal tree that reaches 50 feet or more, grown for its tasty nuts, which are enveloped in leafy, ragged-edged husks. Leaves are handsome and green in summer. Bark is corky and rough. Zones 4-7.

Growing conditions
Filbert grows in full sun or partial shade. It prefers well-drained, loamy soil, tolerates drought and thrives in hot summers and cold winters.

Landscape uses
Filbert makes a good shade tree and accent tree. It can be naturalized in a woodsy border or used as a street tree.

—

Cotinus (ko-TY-nus)
Smoke tree

Deciduous tree that grows 15 to 30 feet tall and may be vase-shaped or rounded in form. It often seems to be enveloped in a smoky haze, which is created by masses of curious, hairy flower stalks that persist long after the inconspicuous greenish yellow flowers have faded in June. Zones 5-8.

Selected species and varieties
C. obovatus, American smoke tree: a small tree, generally 20 to 30 feet tall, that has a rounded crown and orange stems. Bark is gray and scaly. Leaves are a striking blue-green in spring and summer and turn intense shades of yellow and red in autumn. Male plants produce showier flower stalks than females.

Growing conditions
Smoke tree prefers sun but can tolerate partial shade. It thrives on average, well-drained soil. Soil that is too rich or the application of too much fertilizer will encourage foliage production at the expense of flowering.

Landscape uses
Smoke tree may be used as an accent plant in a shrub border.

—

Cottonwood see *Populus*

Crabapple see *Malus*

Crape myrtle see *Lagerstroemia*

Crataegus (kra-TEE-gus)
Hawthorn

Broad-crowned deciduous tree that grows up to 30 feet tall. It has prickly thorns, flowers late in spring or in early summer, and produces small, fleshy fruit that persists into winter. Leaves are lobed and toothed. Bark may be smooth or scaly. Zones 4-9.

Selected species and varieties
C. phaenopyrum, Washington hawthorn: a vase-shaped tree having a spread nearly as wide as it is tall. It bears white blossoms in June and thorns that are up to 3 inches long. Fruits are glossy reddish orange. Leaves are glossy green, turning orange to red in autumn. Zones 4-8. *C. viridis* 'Winter King', winter king hawthorn: similar to Washington hawthorn but with larger fruit and fewer and shorter thorns. Fruit is persistent, but not glossy. Zones 5-7.

Growing conditions
Hawthorns prefer full sun and well-drained loamy soil but adapt well to adverse conditions.

Landscape uses
Hawthorns make good screens, hedges or accent plants.

—

Cryptomeria
(krip-toe-ME-ree-a)

Tall, pyramidal, needle-leaved evergreen native that grows rapidly to 50 or 60 feet in height and 20 to 30 feet in width. Foliage is fine-textured, soft and lush. Bark is reddish brown and shreds in vertical strips. Cones are globe-shaped and approximately 1 inch in diameter. Zones 6-9.

Selected species and varieties
C. japonica, Japanese cedar: foliage is soft and long when young, maturing to shorter, stiffer needles. Needles are awl-shaped and arranged spirally on ropelike drooping branchlets. They are green in spring and summer, turning reddish brown in fall, bronze in winter, or brown if exposed to drying wind. 'Lobbii' is hardier and more compact than the species and holds its green leaf color throughout the winter. 'Yoshino' is columnar and grows to 30 feet tall. It has bronze-green needles in winter.

COTINUS OBOVATUS

CRATAEGUS PHAENOPYRUM

CRYPTOMERIA JAPONICA 'YOSHINO'

CUNNINGHAMIA LANCEOLATA

× CUPRESSOCYPARIS LEYLANDII

CUPRESSUS MACROCARPA

Growing conditions

Japanese cedar grows in sun or partial shade, and in moist, acid soil. It requires protection from wind in open areas and does not tolerate salt spray in coastal areas.

Landscape uses

Japanese cedar makes a good specimen tree and in massed plantings makes a good screen.

—

Cucumber tree see *Magnolia*

—

Cunninghamia
(kun-ing-HAM-ee-a)
China fir

Pyramidal coniferous evergreen that grows to 65 feet or more. It is branched to the ground with wide-spreading, ropelike branches. Cones are 1 to 2 inches long. Needles are 2 to 3 inches long, grayish green, prickly and spirally arranged. Bark is scaly. Zones 7-9.

Selected species and varieties
C. lanceolata: has smaller cones and lighter foliage that is not as sharp to the touch as some species. 'Glauca' has blue-green foliage and is sometimes substituted in the South for northern blue spruce.

Growing conditions
China fir needs full sun but with protection from afternoon winter sun and wind, and moist, loamy, well-drained soil.

Landscape uses
China fir may be used singly as a specimen tree and in massed plantings as a screen.

—

× Cupressocyparis
(kew-press-o-SIP-aris)
Leyland cypress

Narrow pyramidal evergreen that reaches 50 to 70 feet in height. It is a hybrid that combines the rapid growth and resistance to sea winds of one parent, Monterey cypress, with the ability to resist winter damage of its other parent, Nootka false cypress. Zones 7-10.

Selected species and varieties
× *C. leylandii* 'Naylor's Blue': has blue-green leaves. 'Castlewellan' is unusual for being a conifer with yellow foliage.

Growing conditions
Leyland cypress needs full sun and adapts to many soils. It can tolerate salt spray but needs protection from drying and from winter winds.

Landscape uses
Leyland cypress can be used singly as a specimen and in massed plantings as a screen.

—

Cupressus (kew-press-us)
Cypress

Large, long-lived, fragrant evergreen that grows 40 to 90 feet tall. Leaves are scalelike; cones are small and round. Zones 6-9.

Selected species and varieties
C. arizonica, Arizona cypress: has rough, red bark, small blue-green leaves that are fetid when bruised. It is one of the hardier cypresses. Zones 6-8. *C. glabra,* smooth-barked Arizona cypress: similar to Arizona cypress, but the bark shreds annually, exposing smooth, inner red bark. Zones 7-9. *C. macrocarpa,* Monterey cypress: long-lived native Californian that grows along the seaside and reaches 40 feet or more. Trees are pyramidal in youth; as they age, massive limbs widen into an umbrella-like form and eventually sprawl, bend and gnarl in picturesque fashion. Zones 8 and 9. *C. sempervirens,* Italian cypress: a regal Mediterranean that is a slender, formal column 40 to 70 feet or more. It has dark green foliage and thin bark. Zones 8 and 9.

Growing conditions
Arizona cypress, smooth-barked Arizona cypress and Italian cypress need full sun and well-drained soil. All are suitable for mild, dry climates. Monterey cypress needs moist, well-drained soil and does best in the coastal areas of the West; it is difficult to grow on the East Coast.

Landscape uses
Singly cypresses can be used as specimen trees, and in massed plantings they make good screens and windbreaks.

—

Cydonia (sy-DO-nee-a)
Quince

Small deciduous flowering tree that grows to 20 feet in height and bears fragrant, pear-shaped, yellow fruit. Zones 5-9.

Selected species and varieties

C. sinensis, sometimes designated *Pseudocydonia sinensis,* Chinese quince: has a sinewy, knotted trunk, multicolored flaking bark and delicate pale pink to white flowers that appear in May. Foliage is sparse; leaves are oblong and turn yellow to bronzy red in autumn. Zones 6-9.

Growing conditions

Quince will grow in sun or partial shade and in moist or dry soil, but it needs a decidedly acid soil.

Landscape uses

Chinese quince makes a good accent, specimen or patio tree.

—

Cypress see *Cupressocyparis; Cupressus; Taxodium*

Date palm see *Phoenix*

—

Davidia (da-VID-ee-a)

Deciduous 20- to 60-foot-tall ornamental tree with a wide-spreading crown and white, pointed bracts that blossom inconsistently. Zones 6-8.

Selected species and varieties

D. involucrata, dove tree, handkerchief tree: grows 50 to 60 feet. When the tree is mature—about 10 years of age—it has unusual, hooded, floral bracts surrounding a center head of tiny brushlike yellow flowers. The bracts are white and flutter in the breeze, hence the common name, handkerchief tree. They are of unequal length, the lower being about 6 to 8 inches, the upper one 3 to 4 inches. Leaves are heart-shaped at the base and persist until frost turns them brown and kills them.

Growing conditions

Dove tree prefers partial shade and a moist, well-drained soil.

Landscape uses

Dove tree makes a spectacular specimen with its fluttering white bracts.

—

Dawn redwood see *Metasequoia*

Delonix (del-O-nicks)
Poinciana

Deciduous subtropical tree that grows 20 to 40 feet tall with an even wider spread. It produces flamboyant red or yellow flowers in summer and fall. Zone 10.

Selected species and varieties

D. regia, royal poinciana, flame tree, flamboyant, peacock flower: a fast-growing, flat-topped tree with scarlet and yellow flowers that are 3 inches across and have petals shaped like claws. Royal poinciana is one of the showiest flowering trees in the world. The flowers are followed by 2-foot-long pods, which persist long after the leaves drop from the tree. Leaves are fine-textured, ferny and 1 to 2 feet long.

Growing conditions

Royal poinciana demands full sun and frost-free temperatures but is undemanding as to soil. It does not tolerate shade from trees nearby, and it does best along the seashore.

Landscape uses

Royal poinciana makes a striking specimen and can be used as a street tree.

—

Diospyros (die-os-PIE-ros)
Persimmon

Genus of deciduous fruiting trees that grow 35 to 70 feet or more, mostly upright and rounded. Small flowers bloom in spring and are followed in fall by fruit that is fleshy, edible and juicy. Leaves are glossy dark green in summer and change to yellow, orange or purplish red in fall. Zones 4-9.

Selected species and varieties

D. kaki, Japanese persimmon: grows to a height of 20 to 30 feet in a low, rounded, weeping form. It produces tasty, 3- to 4-inch orange to yellow fruit that is sour when green but sweet when ripe. Zones 8 and 9. *D. virginiana,* common persimmon: bears small, fragrant and whitish flowers in June. Fruit is 1 to 1½ inches long and ripens after the first frost. Foliage is 2¼ to 5½ inches long, oval in shape, dense, symmetrical and pendulous. Branches become horizontal as the tree ages. Bark is dark, chunky, blocky and fissured. Zones 4-8.

CYDONIA SINENSIS

DAVIDIA INVOLUCRATA

DELONIX REGIA

DIOSPYROS VIRGINIANA

ELAEAGNUS ANGUSTIFOLIA

ERIOBOTRYA JAPONICA

ERYTHRINA CAFFRA

EUCALYPTUS FICIFOLIA

Growing conditions

Persimmons need full sun. Soil may be alkaline or acid but must be moist and well drained. Both species tolerate city stress.

Landscape uses

Persimmons make good shade trees, and because they are small can be used on patios.

Dogwood see *Cornus*
Douglas fir see *Pseudotsuga*
Dove tree see *Davidia*

Elaeagnus (e-lee-AG-nus)

Deciduous tree that grows 12 to 20 feet in height, has leaves that are covered with minute silvery or brown scales, and bears edible fruit. Zones 2-7.

Selected species and varieties

E. angustifolia, Russian olive: a small and often shrubby, tree that grows in an irregular shape. Its willow-like narrow leaves remain grayish green through summer and autumn. The undersides of the leaves are distinctively silver-scaled. Russian olive's twigs are also silver-scaled and are armed with ½-inch thorns. Fragrant flowers are small, silver outside, yellow inside. Bark is brown and shreds in vertical strips.

Growing conditions

Russian olive must have full sun, but it will tolerate a wide variety of soil types and conditions. The tree requires little maintenance except pruning in spring to keep it tidy.

Landscape uses

Russian olive makes a good accent tree in a border; its silvery foliage makes it stand out among other trees. Several together make a good screen or hedge

---

Elm see *Ulmus*
Empress tree see *Paulownia*
Epaulette tree see *Pterostyrax*

Eriobotrya (air-ee-o-BOT-ree-a)

Broad-leaved evergreen tree that grows 15 to 30 feet in height with

a rounded, open form. Fragrant white flowers are produced in terminal sprays in autumn and winter and are followed by edible yellow-orange fruit in spring. Zones 8-10.

Selected species and varieties

E. deflexa, bronze loquat: has oval leaves that are 5 to 10 inches long and 2 inches wide; they emerge bronze and mature to green. Flowers are approximately ⅝ inch across. Fruit is ¾ inch in diameter. Zones 9 and 10. *E. japonica,* loquat: leaves are 6 to 10 inches long and 1½ to 3 inches wide. Flowers are 1 to 1½ inches long and ⅜ to ¾ inches across. Fruit is 1 to 1½ inches long. 'Golden Nugget' bears fruit in summer. 'Variegata' has leaves that are edged in white.

Growing conditions

Loquats need full sun, well-drained soil and protection from wind.

Landscape uses

Loquats make good accents and patio plants. In the North they should be grown in containers to keep their roots from freezing.

Erythrina (er-i-THRY-na)
Coral tree

Thorny subtropical trees, deciduous and semievergreen, that grow 20 to 60 feet tall and produce large, butterfly-like flowers in dense sprays. Zone 10.

Selected species and varieties

E. caffra, coral tree: semievergreen that grows 20 to 40 feet tall with a broad, spreading crown up to 60 feet in width. Leaves and scarlet flowers emerge at the same time. *E. humeana,* natal coral tree: grows to a height of 20 feet and has stout branchlets.

Growing conditions

Coral tree needs full sun and well-drained soil.

Landscape uses

Coral tree is a good shade tree. In massed plantings natal coral trees make a good hedge.

Eucalyptus (yew-ka-LIP-tus)
Gum tree

Large genus of fast-growing, shallow-rooted evergreens that

range in height from 20 to 100 feet. The leaves are blue-green and fragrant and go through distinct changes in shape; they are round or ovate when young and become elongated as they mature. Flowers bloom in small, feathery heads. Zones 9 and 10.

Selected species and varieties

E. cinerea, silver dollar tree: grows 20 to 50 feet tall. Leaves are coin-shaped and silvery when young. Bark is reddish brown and peels in ribbons on smaller branches. White flowers bloom in spring. Zone 10. *E. ficifolia,* flaming gum, red-flowering gum: small tree that grows to 30 feet with a dense, broad crown and rough, persistent bark. Noted for its showy red flowers, which bloom in midsummer. *E. gunnii,* cider gum: grows to about 45 feet and has small, yellowish white, ball-shaped flowers. Bark is distinctively bicolored, green and white.

Growing conditions

Eucalyptus needs full sun and dry soil. With young trees, cut back on water and fertilizer in fall, or roots may freeze and die.

Landscape uses

Gum trees make good small accent plants. Flaming gum tree serves as a street tree. Cider gum grows fast and provides shade in a few years.

—

Evodia (ee-VO-dee-a)

Deciduous and evergreen trees that grow 25 to 60 feet. They are often aromatic and bear ornamental fruit. Zones 5-8.

Selected species and varieties

E. daniellii, Korean evodia: deciduous tree that grows up to about 30 feet in a spreading, open-branched form. It has large, dark green, compound leaves consisting of seven to 11 leaflets and small, white flower clusters in summer. Fruit capsules are red and hang on into late autumn. Bark is smooth and gray.

Growing conditions

Korean evodia needs full sun and well-drained, moist soil.

Landscape uses

As a small tree, Korean evodia can be container-grown and makes a good accent for a patio.

Fagus (FAY-gus)
Beech

Lofty deciduous shade tree that grows 50 to 100 feet tall and wide. It has a dense, rounded head, oval leaves that are toothed and pointed, and smooth, light gray bark. Spring flowers are followed by small triangular nuts enclosed in prickly cases. Zones 3-9.

Selected species and varieties

F. grandifolia, American beech: grows to a height of 50 to 70 feet or more with a short trunk, conspicuous surface roots and a wide-spreading crown. Leaves are 2 to 6 inches long and sharply toothed and turn golden copper in autumn. Zones 3-8.

F. sylvatica, European beech: grows 70 to 80 feet tall. Has smaller leaves, 2 to 4 inches long, which turn a russet color in autumn. Branches are low and leafy, and often sweep the ground. Zones 5-8. The cultivar 'Asplenifolia' has graceful, fernlike leaves that turn golden brown in autumn. 'Dawyckii' is column-shaped; it grows 80 feet or more in height and only 10 feet in width. 'Laciniata' has deeply saw-toothed leaves. 'Pendula', weeping beech: has branches that sweep down at angles of 60° to 45°. 'Riversii', Rivers purple beech: has leaves that are deep purple in color. 'Rotundifolia', roundleaf beech: has a pyramidal shape and dense, dark green, rounded foliage that persists in winter.

Growing conditions

Beech does best in full sun and in moist, well-drained acid soil.

Landscape uses

Its great height and massive spread make beech a spectacular specimen. It provides shade so dense that few plants will grow beneath it.

—

False cypress
see *Chamaecyparis*

Fan palm see *Livistona*

—

Ficus (FY-kus)
Fig

Broad-leaved evergreen and deciduous trees that grow 10 to 75 feet tall. They have short, stout branches that grow downward to the ground and take root, thus de-

EVODIA DANIELLII

FAGUS GRANDIFOLIA

FAGUS SYLVATICA 'PENDULA'

FICUS BENJAMINA

FIRMIANA SIMPLEX

FRANKLINIA ALATAMAHA

FRAXINUS EXCELSIOR 'AUREA'

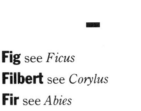

FRAXINUS ORNUS

veloping into additional stems. The foliage discharges a milky sap when bruised. Zones 8-10.

Selected species and varieties
F. benjamina, weeping fig: evergreen that reaches 30 to 50 feet in height in approximately 30 years. Leaves are leathery, pointed and 5 inches long. Bark is smooth and gray. Zone 10.

Growing conditions
Weeping fig prefers filtered sun and loamy garden soil.

Landscape uses
Weeping fig can be used as a specimen tree or lawn accent in mild climates. In temperate or cold climates it can be container-grown for the patio and brought indoors for the winter.

—

Fig see *Ficus*

Filbert see *Corylus*

Fir see *Abies*

—

Firmiana (firm-ee-AY-na)

Fast-growing deciduous ornamental tree that grows to 75 feet and has large, usually lobed, leaves. Zones 7-9.

Selected species and varieties
F. simplex, Chinese parasol tree: a roundheaded tree that grows 45 to 50 feet tall. It has smooth green bark, whorled branches, large palmate leaves up to 12 inches across, and small but showy flowers in upright sprays. Small, wrinkled, green fruit capsules open before they are ripe and separate into leaflike pods, discharging a liquid as they open.

Growing conditions
Chinese parasol tree needs full sun, reasonably moist soil and protection from wind.

Landscape uses
Chinese parasol tree makes a good shade, accent or street tree.

—

Flamboyant see *Delonix*

Flame tree see *Delonix*

Floss silk tree see *Chorisia*

Franklinia (frank-LIN-ee-a)

Deciduous tree that grows 10 to 30 feet tall with multiple trunks and upright-spreading branches. Bark is fissured. Foliage is shiny and dark green, and it changes to shades of orange and red in fall. Woody, capsuled fruit produces flat, wingless seed. Zones 6-8.

Selected species and varieties
F. alatamaha, Franklin tree: bears fragrant, white, five-petaled blossoms that are frilly and cupped, and nearly 3 inches across. They bloom from late summer to fall.

Growing conditions
Franklin tree flowers best in full sun. It needs moist, well-drained, acid soil.

Landscape uses
Because it blossoms late when few ornamentals are flowering and has attractive bark, Franklin tree is well suited for use as an accent or a specimen tree.

—

Fraxinus (FRAK-sah-nus)
Ash

Tall, usually deciduous, rapid-growing, round-crowned shade tree that grows to 80 feet. Clusters of small flowers appear in early spring and are followed by clusters of 1-inch paddle-shaped winged seeds that cling until fall. Leaves are generally compound with up to 11 leaflets. Zones 2-9.

Selected species and varieties
F. americana, white ash: grows 50 to 80 feet. Leaves turn orange to purple in fall. Bark is diamond-patterned and gray on mature trees. Zones 3-9. 'Autumn Purple' grows to 60 feet. It is a cultivar bred to be nonfruiting and litterless. It has glossy deep green leaves that turn reddish purple to mahogany in fall. 'Rosehill' is a seedless ash that grows to 50 feet. Its leaves turn bronze-red in fall. Zones 5-9. *F. excelsior,* European ash: grows 70 to 80 feet tall with a 60- to 90-foot spread. Lower branches curve upward. Leaves are dark green in summer and drop when they are still green or after fading to yellow. Zones 4-6. 'Aurea' grows slowly and is noted for its yellow twigs, yellow older bark and yellow fall color. 'Hessei' has a straight trunk and flat-topped crown. Leaves,

unlike most ash leaves, are simple, ovate, pointed and deeply toothed. Zone 4. *F. ornus,* flowering ash: grows to 40 to 50 feet and has small, but profuse, fragrant white flowers in long, dense clusters, which distinguish it from other ash trees. Zones 5-7. *F. pennsylvanica,* green ash: is distinguished from white ash by its narrow crown and tan diamond-patterned bark. Zones 3-9. 'Marshall's Seedless' is a hardy, nonfruiting cultivar that grows 50 to 60 feet. 'Summit' is a seedless cultivar that is fast growing, with upright branches and fine-textured foliage. *F. uhdei,* shamel ash, evergreen ash: grows fast to 30 to 50 feet. It is densely branched and has glossy leaves. Zone 9.

Growing conditions
Most ashes adapt to any soil if they get full sun.

Landscape uses
Ashes make good specimen trees and provide dense shade.

—

Frijolito see *Sophora*

—

Ginkgo (GINK-o)
Ginkgo, maidenhair tree

Deciduous tree that grows to 80 feet in an irregular form. It has exotic fan-shaped leaves that are often deeply notched at the center of the outer margin. Zones 4-8.

Selected species and varieties
G. biloba, maidenhair tree: grows between 30 to 80 feet tall. Leaves appear on short branchlets and turn bright yellow in autumn. Bark is gray-brown and ridged. Male and female flowers are produced on separate trees; female trees are undesirable because the seeds have an unpleasant odor. 'Autumn Gold' is a nonfruiting cultivar that is medium-size. Zones 5-8. 'Fastigiata', sentry ginkgo, is narrowly pyramidal in form.

Growing conditions
Ginkgo will grow in full sun or partial shade and needs well-drained, moist, slightly acid soil.

Landscape uses
Ginkgo makes a good specimen tree and provides dappled shade.

Gleditsia (gle-DIT-see-a)
Honey locust

Fast-growing deciduous tree that grows 30 to 70 feet tall with a broad, open crown and a short trunk. Branches are spreading, sometimes drooping; branchlets are slender and armed with long, pointed, forked spines. Pods are long and narrow and contain a sweet, gummy sap. Zones 3-9.

Selected species and varieties
G. triacanthos inermis, thornless honey locust: has smooth stems and delicate, lacy, compound foliage that provides filtered shade. Bark is brown and furrowed. Fragrant greenish flower clusters appear in May. Foliage turns yellow in fall. The fruit is a straplike pod that forms in late summer and twists spirally before it falls. 'Moraine' is a sterile cultivar that produces no pods. 'Shademaster' is a podless cultivar with a strong central trunk and ascending branches. 'Skyline' has an upright shape and leaves that turn gold in fall. 'Sunburst' grows 30 to 35 feet tall and has an upright spreading shape. Foliage emerges yellow in early summer and then turns green, but it retains a tinge of yellow at the twig tips. Zones 4-9.

Growing conditions
Honey locust needs full sun and prefers alkaline soil. It tolerates flooding and is resistant to wind damage, highway salting and urban pollution.

Landscapes uses.
Honey locust makes a good specimen tree. It provides dappled shade; grass and ground cover will grow beneath it.

—

Golden chain tree
see *Laburnum*

Golden larch see *Pseudolarix*

Golden rain tree
see *Koelreuteria*

Golden shower tree see *Cassia*

Green ebony see *Jacaranda*

Gum see *Eucalyptus*

—

Gymnocladus
(jim-no-CLA-dus)

Deciduous tree that grows 50 to 75 feet, occasionally to 100 feet, with a

GINKGO BILOBA

GLEDITSIA TRIACANTHOS INERMIS 'SHADEMASTER'

GYMNOCLADUS DIOICUS

HALESIA MONTICOLA

IDESIA POLYCARPA

ILEX × 'NELLIE R. STEVENS'

spread of 40 feet. It has stout branches and feather-like foliage. Fragrant flower clusters appear in spring. Zones 4-8.

Selected species and varieties
G. dioicus, Kentucky coffee tree: generally grows to 60 to 75 feet, but can reach 90 feet. Leaves are 36 inches long, 24 inches wide and doubly compound, with many leaflets per leaf. Bark is scaly, ridged and dark gray to black. Flowers are greenish white. On female trees, thick, reddish brown pods appear in fall and persist into winter.

Growing conditions
Kentucky coffee tree grows in full sun or partial shade. It prefers fertile soil but tolerates dry soil. It also tolerates urban pollution.

Landscape uses
Kentucky coffee tree makes a good specimen tree on land large enough to accommodate it. Male trees, because they produce no pods, may be used as street trees.

—

Hackberry see *Celtis*

—

Halesia (hal-EE-zha)
Silverbell, snowdrop tree

Deciduous ornamental, 20 to 80 feet tall, with drooping flower clusters that form on the previous year's wood, and four-winged fruit that emerges green and ripens to brown. Zones 4-8.

Selected species and varieties
H. carolina, Carolina silverbell: grows 20 to 30 feet in a wide-spreading, rounded or irregular form. Long, white, bell-shaped flower clusters appear in late April and early May. Leaves are bright green, simple and finely toothed, and turn yellow in fall. Bark is gray to brown and vertically furrowed. *H. diptera,* two-winged silverbell: 20- to 30-foot tree with low-branching, multiple-stem form. Fruit has two wings instead of four. Zones 6-8. *H. monticola,* mountain silverbell: grows up to 80 feet and is similar to Carolina silverbell but has larger flowers and fruits. Zone 5.

Growing conditions
Silverbell grows in full sun or partial shade and moist, well-drained, acid soil. It needs protection from wind.

Landscape uses
Silverbell makes a good accent on a patio. It may also be used in a woodland border and as an understory plant—that is, interspersed among taller trees.

—

Handkerchief tree see *Davidia*

Hawthorn see *Crataegus*

Hazelnut see *Corylus*

Hemlock see *Tsuga*

Hickory see *Carya*

Holly see *Ilex*

Honey locust see *Gleditsia*

Hop hornbeam see *Ostrya*

Hornbeam see *Carpinus*

Horse chestnut see *Aesculus*

Horsetail tree see *Casuarina*

—

Idesia (eye-DEE-see-a)
Iigiri tree

Deciduous tree that grows 40 to 50 feet tall. It has fragrant clusters of flowers in late spring and ornamental fruit in fall. Zones 8 and 9; marginally, Zone 7.

Selected species and varieties
I. polycarpa, iigiri tree: leaves are heart-shaped and have widely spaced teeth. Flowers are 10-inch-long clusters. Fruit is red and dangles from the branchlets of female trees like small bunches of pea-size grapes in fall. Branches spread horizontally in tiers.

Growing conditions
Iigiri tree grows in full sun or partial shade and in slightly acid, loamy soil.

Landscape uses
Iigiri tree makes a good shade tree on a lawn, a patio or a street.

—

Iigiri see *Idesia*

—

Ilex (EYE-leks)
Holly

Genus of deciduous and evergreen trees, 10 to 50 feet tall, that grow all over the world. They are pyramidal in shape and have leathery leaves. Male and female trees bear red or yellow berry-like fruit in fall; trees of both sexes must be planted together to produce. Zones 3-9.

Selected species and varieties
I. aquifolium, English holly: grows to 20 feet and has leaves that are wavy-edged and spiny when the tree is young; as the tree ages the leaves on its upper branches lose their spines and become smooth. Zones 6-8. *I. × attenuata* 'Fosteri' #2 and #3, Foster holly: both are compact, have glossy green, small leaves with spiny edges, and abundant fruit. Zones 6-9. *I. latifolia,* lusterleaf holly: grows up to 40 feet tall. Leaves are glossy and spineless. Fruit is red and occurs in dense clusters. Zones 7 and 8. *I. ×* 'Nellie R. Stevens': fast-growing cultivar bred to produce fruit without the assistance of a male. It grows 25 feet tall and its leaves have only two to three teeth on each side. Zones 6-9. *I. opaca,* American holly: slow-growing tree that reaches 40 to 50 feet. Form is pyramidal in youth and becomes irregular with age. Branches are short and crooked. Leaves are ovate and spiny-toothed. Fruit is red in fall. Zones 7-9. *I. pedunculosa,* longstalk holly: grows to 20 feet or more, with shiny, pointed, dark green, spineless leaves and red berries. Zones 5-7. *I. vomitoria* 'Pendula', weeping yaupon: grows to 20 feet in a weeping form and bears abundant scarlet fruit that persists into spring. Zones 8 and 9.

Growing conditions
Hollies grow in full sun or partial shade. They need moist, well-drained soil and protection from winter sun and winds.

Landscape uses
Hollies can be used as specimens or accents, and in hedges and borders.

—

Jacaranda (jack-a-RAND-a)
Green ebony

Tropical deciduous tree, 10 to 60 feet tall, grown for its fragrant blue to violet blossoms, which float to the ground and carpet the base of the tree. Zone 10.

Selected species and varieties
J. acutifolia: multiple-trunked, fast-growing tree that reaches 40 feet. Trumpet-shaped flowers oc-
cur in loose clusters at the ends of branches that form a leafless crown. Leaves are fernlike, 1½ to 2 feet long, and composed of hundreds of ¼-inch leaflets that cast a dappled shade. Disc-shaped, 2-inch-long seedpods hang on the tree for most of the year. *J. mimosifolia:* grows up to 50 feet tall. Leaves persist until early spring. Flower clusters are nearly 8 inches long.

Growing conditions
Green ebony does best in full sun and well-drained, sandy, acid soil. It should be planted in a sheltered spot, away from piercing winds.

Landscape uses
Green ebony is suitable for use as a specimen, an accent or a street tree.

—

Japanese cedar see *Cryptomeria*
Japanese pagoda tree
see *Sophora*
Japanese umbrella tree
see *Sciadopitys*

—

Juglans (JOO-glanz)
Walnut

Deciduous shade tree that reaches 30 to 70 feet in height. It has edible nuts and compound leaves that are aromatic when crushed. Zones 3-8.

Selected species and varieties
J. cinerea, butternut, white walnut: grows 40 to 60 feet tall with a spread of 30 to 50 feet. The trunk is short and Y-shaped, and supports a broad, rounded crown. Bark has whitish ridges and grayish black furrows. Nuts occur in clusters of two to five. Zones 3-7. *J. nigra,* black walnut: an imposing shade tree that grows 50 to 70 feet tall. Bark is dark brown and deeply grooved in a diamond-shaped pattern. Catkins open in spring; nuts ripen in October or November. Zones 5-7. 'Laciniata' has finely cut foliage. *J. regia,* English walnut: grows 40 to 60 feet tall with a spread nearly as wide. Silvery gray bark fissures with age. Zones 5-8.

Growing conditions
Walnuts do well in full sun or partial shade and in moist, well-drained soil.

Landscape uses
Walnuts make good specimen trees

JACARANDA MIMOSIFOLIA

JUGLANS NIGRA

JUNIPERUS CHINENSIS 'KAIZUKA'

JUNIPERUS VIRGINIANA

KOELREUTERIA PANICULATA

on property large enough to accommodate them. They are not recommended for small gardens because their roots exude juglone, a substance that is toxic to some garden plants.

Juneberry see *Amelanchier*

Juniper see *Juniperus*

Juniperus (joo-NIP-er-us)
Juniper

Pyramidal coniferous evergreens that grow 15 to 65 feet tall. Foliage may be needle-like or scalelike. Cones on male trees are cylindrical; those on female trees are globe-shaped. Because the genus is so varied in size, form and foliage color, it is the most widely planted group of evergreens in home gardens. Zones 3-9.

Selected species and varieties
J. chinensis, Chinese juniper: grows to 50 to 60 feet in height with a spread of 15 to 20 feet. Foliage is green to blue-green to grayish green; on young trees it is sharp, but as the tree ages it becomes scalelike and blunt. 'Columnaris' is a tall, narrow tree that grows to 33 feet tall with a spread only one-fourth of its height. It has a loose branching habit. Foliage is deep green and awl-shaped. 'Kaizuka', Hollywood juniper: grows to a height of 15 feet with branches that spiral upward and bright green foliage. Zones 6-9.

J. scopulorum, Rocky Mountain juniper, Colorado red cedar: a narrow, pyramidal tree that grows slowly to 30 or 40 feet in height and 3 to 15 feet in width. It often has multiple main stems. Bark is reddish brown or gray, and it shreds. Foliage has a silvery blue cast and retains its color throughout the winter. Cones are dark blue and ripen in two years. Zones 3-7.

J. virginiana, eastern red cedar: grows to a height of 40 feet or more. Foliage is medium green in summer and turns purplish or brown in winter; it is awl-shaped and pointed when young and becomes scalelike and blunt when mature. Zones 2-9. The cultivar 'Canaerti' grows 20 to 25 feet tall. It differs from the species in that it holds its deep green color year round. Foliage is tufted; cones are bright blue. Zones 3-8. 'Glauca', silver red juniper: grows in a narrow, columnar form to 25 feet. Foliage is fine-textured, silver-blue in spring and silver-green in the growing season.

Growing conditions
Junipers grow in full sun to partial shade. Moist to dry, well-drained sandy soil is best, but junipers are easy to grow and adapt to a variety of conditions.

Landscape uses
Junipers used singly make good specimens and massed together make good screens and backgrounds for other plants.

Katsura tree see *Cercidiphyllum*

Kentucky coffee tree see *Gymnocladus*

Koelreuteria
(kol-ru-TEE-ree-a)
Golden rain tree

Rapidly growing deciduous tree that reaches 45 to 60 feet. It has feather-like leaves and 12- to 15-inch clusters of small, yellow flowers that fall to the ground. Zones 5-9.

Selected species and varieties
K. bipinnata: upright, round-headed tree that grows to 60 feet. Seedpods emerge pink and dry to tan. Zones 7-9. *K. elegans,* Chinese flame tree: grows to 60 feet with a flat-topped, spreading crown. Seedpods are bright orange-red and resemble Chinese lanterns. Zone 9. *K. paniculata,* panicled golden rain tree: round-headed tree that grows to 30 feet tall and spreads as wide. Seedpods are balloon-like in shape and greenish in color. They turn yellow, then brown, in fall. Zones 5-7.

Growing conditions
Golden rain tree grows in full sun to partial shade and in well-drained soil. It adapts to a wide range of conditions and tolerates urban pollution.

Landscape uses
Golden rain trees make good specimens, and are also suited for use as shade and street trees.

Laburnum (la-BUR-num)

Small deciduous tree that grows 10 to 30 feet tall and is noted for its 20-inch pendulous clusters of 1-inch yellow flowers. Bark is smooth, dark olive green to brown with black patches. Leaves are composed of three small oval leaflets. Pods are brown and leathery and persist until winter. Zones 4-7.

Selected species and varieties
L. × watereri, golden chain tree: grows 10 to 15 feet with yellow blossoms that dangle like chains from its branches. The tree may be rounded or vase-shaped and is open in form. Foliage is bright blue-green in summer. Zones 5-7. 'Vossii' was bred to have a dense form. Zones 6 and 7.

Growing conditions
Golden chain tree grows in full sun or partial shade and in well-drained soil. It needs shelter from drying winds and from hot afternoon sun, especially in winter.

Landscape uses
Golden chain tree is best used as an accent tree in a massed planting. Plant it with discretion; its seeds and leaves are toxic.

Lagerstroemia
(lay-ger-STREAM-ee-a)
Crape myrtle

Small to large deciduous trees ranging in height from 10 to 60 feet. They have multiple stems and broad, spreading crowns, and they bloom profusely in white and a broad range of pinks, reds and purples. Flower petals are crinkled like crepe paper. Zones 7-10.

Selected species and varieties
L. indica: grows to about 20 feet and has smooth, exfoliating bark that exposes gray-brown underbark. Flowers bloom recurrently from July through September. Leaves are elliptic to oblong, yellowish green to bronze when emerging, then dark green in summer, and yellow, orange or red in autumn. Zones 7-9. 'Muskogee' grows up to 21 feet high and 15 feet wide. Bark is medium brown, leaves are green in summer and turn red in autumn, flowers are pale lavender. 'Natchez' grows up to 21 feet high and 21 feet wide. Bark is dark cinnamon brown and mottled, flowers are white, and leaves turn orange and red in fall. 'Tuscarora' grows up to 15 feet high and 15 feet wide with leaves that emerge red-tinged, turn dark green in summer and then orange-red in fall. Flowers are dark coral pink.

Growing conditions
Crape myrtle needs full sun; it does not flower well in shade. It will grow in any well-drained soil but prefers slightly acid loam. Once established, it tolerates drought. Encourage repeated blooming by removing spent flowers.

Landscape uses
Crape myrtle makes a fine specimen or border plant. It provides dappled shade; grass and other ground covers can grow underneath its canopy.

Larch see *Larix*

Larix (LAIR-icks)
Larch

Deciduous conifer that grows 40 to 90 feet tall. Leaves are needle-like, spirally arranged and clustered on spur branches. Bark is reddish brown and peels. Zones 1-7.

Selected species and varieties
L. decidua, European larch: grows 70 to 75 feet in height and 25 to 30 feet in spread. It has lacy, soft green, needle-like foliage that turns yellow in fall, and cones that have wavy scales. Zones 2-6. *L. kaempferi,* Japanese larch: fast-growing tree that reaches 70 to 90 feet tall. Leaves are pale bluish green in summer, gold in fall and have two whitish bands on the undersides. Larch cones have scales that turn back at the tops, giving a rosette-like appearance. Zones 4-7.

Growing conditions
Larches need full sun and moist, acid soil.

Landscape uses
Larches make good specimens in areas large enough to accommodate them. They may also be used as screens and naturalized in woodland borders.

Laurel see *Laurus; Persea*

LABURNUM × WATERERI 'VOSSII'

LAGERSTROEMIA INDICA

LARIX DECIDUA

LAURUS NOBILIS

LIQUIDAMBAR STYRACIFLUA

LIRIODENDRON TULIPIFERA

Laurus (LAW-rus)
Laurel, sweet bay

Broad-leaved evergreen that grows 10 to 40 feet tall. Foliage is dense, leathery and aromatic. Zones 8-10.

Selected species and varieties
L. nobilis, bay laurel, sweet bay: grows slowly to 30 feet tall. Leaves are oval, dark green, pointed and glossy. Inconspicuous greenish white flowers appear in spring and are followed by small dark berries. Zones 8-10.

Growing conditions
Laurel will grow in full sun or partial shade and needs well-drained, moist soil. Suckers need to be pruned annually.

Landscape uses
Laurel can be espaliered on a trellis or a wall. In northern regions, it can be container-grown on a patio in summer and moved indoors in the winter.

Leyland cypress
see *Cupressocyparis*

Lilac see *Syringa*

Limetree see *Tilia*

Linden see *Tilia*

Liquidambar (lik-wid-AM-bar)
Sweet gum

Deciduous tree that grows 25 to 80 feet tall with star-shaped leaves having five to seven lobes and toothed edges. Fruits are woody, spiny capsules containing a gummy sap that hang from long stems. Bark is ridged and resembles cork. Zones 5-9.

Selected species and varieties
L. styraciflua: grows 70 to 80 feet tall. The tree is symmetrical and pyramidal in shape when young but develops a rounded crown with age. Leaves hang on the tree until late in autumn and turn rich shades of yellow, purple and red. Zones 6-9.

Growing conditions
Sweet gum grows in full sun to partial shade and needs moist, well-drained acid soil. It tolerates saltwater spray if sheltered from strong winds.

Landscape uses
Sweet gum makes a good specimen and shade tree.

Liriodendron
(leer-ee-oh-DEN-dron)
Tulip tree

Massive deciduous tree that grows 25 to 30 feet tall in eight years and may eventually reach more than 100 feet with a spread half as wide. It branches high on the trunk and is noted for its upright, tulip-like flowers in spring. Zones 5-9.

Selected species and varieties
L. tulipifera, tulip tree, yellow poplar, tulip magnolia, tulip poplar, whitewood: grows 60 to 90 feet tall. The crown is conical in youth and becomes oval with age. Leaves are 5 inches across, lobed and blunt along the top edge. They turn yellow in autumn. When the tree reaches 10 years of age, it produces tulip-like blossoms that are yellowish green with a deep orange blotch at the base of the petals. Fruits are slim, winged and conelike, and persist into winter. Bark is ridged and furrowed. The cultivar 'Aureomarginatum' has leaves that are variegated with yellow or greenish yellow margins.

Growing conditions
Tulip tree grows in full sun. It requires moist, well-drained, slightly acid soil that is deep enough to accommodate the tree's massive root system.

Landscape uses
Tulip tree is a good specimen tree in an area large enough to contain its enormous root system and broad branching habit.

Live oak see *Quercus*

Livistona (liv-i-STO-na)
Fan palm

Tropical ornamental evergreen that grows 65 feet tall. Leaf spread is 6 feet across. Zones 9 and 10.

Selected species and varieties
L. chinensis, Chinese fountain plant: grows to 30 feet or more, with a thick trunk from which a cluster of glossy green, fan-shaped leaves emerge. The lower part of

the leaf stalk, which can grow up to 6 feet long, is armed with spines that disappear with age. Flowers are clustered, and fruit is metallic blue, ovate and about 1 inch long.

Growing conditions
Fan palm needs partial shade, moist soil and a humid environment.

Landscape uses
Fan palm makes a good specimen or accent tree. Young trees can be container-grown for use on patios.

Locust see *Robinia*

Loquat see *Eriobotrya*

Maackia (MACK-ee-a)

Deciduous tree that grows 20 to 70 feet tall. Leaves are feather-like with paired leaflets. Flowers are white and fragrant, and occur in dense, upright sprays. Zones 3-7.

Selected species and varieties
M. amurensis, Amur maackia: roundheaded tree, up to 30 feet, with pea-shaped flowers that bloom in July. Leaves are grayish green when young and turn dark as they mature. Bark is bronze and peels. Zones 3-7. *M. chinensis:* similar to Amur maakia, but its new growth is silvery. Zones 4-7.

Growing conditions
Maackia needs full sun and loose, well-drained soil and pruning when young. It is extraordinarily hardy and can withstand temperatures as low as −30° F.

Landscape uses
Maackia makes a good specimen tree or lawn accent.

Madrone see *Arbutus*

Magnolia (mag-NO-lee-a)

Genus of deciduous or evergreen trees, 20 to 80 feet tall, having large showy blossoms and large, leathery, dark green leaves. Zones 4-9.

Selected species and varieties
M. acuminata, cucumber tree: deciduous tree that grows to 50 to 80 feet tall or more, and nearly as wide. It has massive, wide-spreading branches, is pyramidal in youth and becomes broadly rounded in age. Leaves are 4 to 10 inches in length. Flowers are 3 inches long, loosely cup-shaped and yellowish green. Fruit is knobby, cucumber-like and slits open in early fall to reveal red, pea-size seeds that dangle on slender threads. Zones 4-8. *M. grandiflora,* southern magnolia, bull bay: broad-leaved evergreen that grows 60 to 80 feet in height and 30 to 50 feet in spread with a low-branching habit. The tree may take 15 to 20 years to blossom; flowers, when they emerge, are white, nearly 1 foot in diameter and fragrant. Leaves are 4 to 10 inches long, ovate and pointed. Zones 6-9. 'Glenn St. Mary' flowers at a younger age than others of the species. 'Lanceolata' is narrower in form than others. Leaves are narrow and rust-colored on the undersides. *M. heptapeta,* Yulan magnolia: deciduous tree that grows 30 to 40 feet tall and nearly as wide. Flowers are 5 to 6 inches in diameter. Zones 6-9. *M.* × 'Elizabeth': flower buds are tapered and reveal clear yellow petals as they open. *M.* × *loebneri,* Loebner magnolia: deciduous, compact tree, 20 to 30 feet tall, that casts dense shade. Flowers have 12 white to blush pink petals, and the bark is silver-gray. 'Merrill' has 15 white petals per blossom. *M.* × *soulangiana,* saucer magnolia: deciduous tree that grows 20 to 30 feet tall. Flowers are 5 to 10 inches in diameter, white inside and tinged with pink or purple outside. Bark is smooth and gray. 'Alexandrina' flowers earlier in spring than other cultivars; 'Brozzonii' is the last to flower.

Growing conditions
Magnolias grow in full sun or partial shade. They need deep, moist, slightly acid, well-drained soil and protection from wind. To maintain shape, prune trees after they have flowered.

Landscape uses
Magnolias make spectacular specimen trees where there is room to accommodate their deep roots and broad-spreading branches.

Maidenhair tree see *Ginkgo*

LIVISTONA CHINENSIS

MAACKIA AMURENSIS

MAGNOLIA × SOULANGIANA

MALUS FLORIBUNDA

METASEQUOIA GLYPTOSTROBOIDES

MORUS ALBA

Malus (MAY-lus)
Flowering crabapple

Deciduous flowering tree that grows 15 to 25 feet tall. It produces abundant clusters of white to pink or purplish single flowers, and yellow, orange, or red to purple fruits that are 2 inches or smaller. Some species bloom only in alternate years. Zones 2-6.

Selected species and varieties
M. 'Adams': annual-bearing crabapple that grows to about 20 feet tall and 20 feet wide with a rounded, densely branched outline. Leaves are green with a reddish tint when they open; flower buds are red, fading to soft pink; fruit is red and persistent. M. floribunda, Japanese flowering crabapple: grows to 15 to 25 feet tall and just as wide. It has a rounded, arching outline, is densely branched and has fine-textured foliage. Fragrant pink to red buds bloom in midspring, fade to white as the blossoms open, and are followed by red or yellow fruit. 'Red Jade' grows 15 feet tall or more. It has graceful, slender, weeping branches. Leaves are glossy, vibrant green; flowers are white and profuse. Fruit appears annually, is bright, red, showy and persistent. 'Snowdrift' grows 15 to 20 feet tall in a dense, rounded form. Red buds open to white flowers. Fruit appears annually and is orange-red. M. sieboldii zumi 'Calocarpa', redbud crab: grows to 25 feet tall. It has a rounded crown, spreading, drooping branchlets and a dense canopy of dark green foliage. Bright red flower buds open to fragrant white blossoms and are followed by glossy red fruits that are persistent.

Growing conditions
Crabapples need full sun for best flowering and fruit. They should have well-drained, moist, acid soil, and they need pruning in spring. Of all flowering fruit trees, crabapples are the easiest to grow and the most cold-hardy.

Landscape uses
Singly crabapples make good specimen trees, and in massed plantings they make good borders. 'Red Jade' can be container-grown on a patio.

—

Manzanita see Arbutus
Maple see Acer

Mescal bean see Sophora

—

Metasequoia
(met-a-see-KWOY-a)
Dawn redwood

Deciduous tree that grows 70 to 80 feet or more. It has long, feathery needles. Zones 5-8.

Selected species and varieties
M. glyptostroboides: grows in a pyramidal outline. Foliage is green in summer and turns orange-brown to red-brown in autumn. Cones are globular in shape, about ¾ inch across, and hang from long stalks. Bark is reddish brown and peels in long, narrow strips.

Growing conditions
Dawn redwood needs full sun and grows best in deep, moist, slightly acid soil.

Landscape uses
Dawn redwood makes a good specimen tree on properties that are large enough to accommodate its great size.

—

Mimosa see Albizia
Monkey puzzle see Araucaria

—

Morus (MO-rus)
Mulberry

Deciduous tree that grows 30 to 80 feet tall. It has a rounded form and stout, spreading branches. Zones 4-9.

Selected species and varieties
M. alba, white mulberry: grows 30 to 50 feet tall and has glossy leaves that are toothed and irregularly lobed. Greenish flowers emerge in April as loose, hanging catkins and are followed by edible fleshy whitish to pink to purple fruit. Bark is yellow-orange to brown and irregularly fissured. 'Kingan' is drought-resistant. 'Stribling' is fruitless and the leaves turn bright yellow in fall. 'Urbana' is also fruitless and has a weeping form.

Growing conditions
Mulberry grows in full sun to partial shade and adapts to any good soil. It needs pruning to maintain its form.

Landscape uses
Mulberry makes a good speci-

men tree. 'Kingan' and 'Stribling' make good shade trees because they do not bear fruit that might cause litter.

Mountain ash see *Sorbus*

Mountain ebony see *Bauhinia*

Mulberry see *Morus*

Musclewood see *Carpinus*

Norfolk Island pine see *Araucaria*

Nyssa (NIS-sa)
Tupelo

Deciduous tree that grows 25 to 75 feet tall with a spread half as wide. It has a tall domed crown and its leaves turn scarlet in fall. Zones 5-9.

Selected species and varieties
N. sylvatica, pepperidge, sour gum, black gum, black tupelo: grows 30 to 50 feet tall or more. It has horizontal branching that gives it a spreading form in youth but becomes somewhat weeping and irregular with age. Leaves are bright, shiny, dark green in summer and change to bright yellow, orange, scarlet or purple in fall. Female flowers are small, greenish white and borne in clusters. Fruit is fleshy, blue-black and bitter-tasting. Older trees have dark, furrowed bark.

Growing conditions
Tupelo grows in full sun to partial shade. It must have deep, acid soil and a moist location that is sheltered from winds.

Landscape uses
Tupelo makes a good specimen, shade tree or street tree. It can also be naturalized in a woodsy border.

Oak see *Quercus*

Olea (OH-lee-a)
Olive

Small broad-leaved evergreen tree that grows 25 to 30 feet tall. It is multiple-stemmed and spreads as wide as it is tall. Zones 8-10.

Selected species and varieties
O. europaea, European olive: has gnarled and furrowed stems. Leaves are feathery and silvery gray-green. It produces clusters of small, fragrant, yellow flowers in spring and edible black olives in fall.

Growing conditions
Olive thrives in hot, sunny, dry areas but needs some winter chilling—to 50° F or lower—for flowers to form. The tree is best grown in deep, fertile loam.

Landscape uses
Olive makes a good accent or shade tree. Young trees can be container-grown for use on patios.

Olive see *Olea*

Orchid tree see *Bauhinia*

Osmanthus (oz-MAN-thus)

Fragrant, broad-leaved evergreen tree that grows to 45 feet. It has a short trunk and a dense, rounded crown. It belongs to the olive family. Zones 6-9.

Selected species and varieties
O. fragrans, sweet olive: grows 20 to 30 feet tall. Leaves are leathery, oval-shaped and may be finely toothed. Small, white, sweet-scented flowers bloom year round. Zones 8 and 9.

Growing conditions
Sweet olive grows in full sun or partial shade and in moist, acid soil.

Landscape uses
Singly sweet olive makes a good specimen tree; several together make a good border.

Ostrya (OS-tree-a)
Hop hornbeam

Deciduous ornamental tree that grows slowly 25 to 40 feet tall. It has a dense canopy of leaves and produces fruit in clusters of inflated pods. Zones 3-8.

Selected species and varieties
O. virginiana, American hop hornbeam, ironwood: leaves are 1½ to 5 inches long and toothed, and may be ovate, rounded or heart-shaped. They are dark green in summer and

NYSSA SYLVATICA

OLEA EUROPAEA

OSMANTHUS FRAGRANS

OSTRYA VIRGINIANA

OXYDENDRUM ARBOREUM

PARROTIA PERSICA

PAULOWNIA TOMENTOSA

PERSEA BORBONIA

change to yellow in fall. Stems are reddish brown. Flowers are 1- to 2-inch-long clusters, greenish in color, and open early in spring. Fruit clusters are 1½ to 2½ inches long, ⅔ to 1½ inches wide and greenish yellow.

Growing conditions
Hop hornbeam grows in full sun to partial shade and in many different types of soil. It cannot tolerate salt.

Landscape uses
Hop hornbeam makes a good specimen tree. It can also be interspersed as an understory plant among taller trees.

—

Oxydendrum
(ok-see-DEN-drum)
Sourwood, sorrel tree

Deciduous slow-growing tree that generally reaches 25 to 30 feet; over a long period of time it may attain 50 to 75 feet. It has multiple stems and a pyramidal crown. It is ornamental in four seasons. It has glossy, leathery leaves in spring; white, bell-shaped flowers in summer; scarlet foliage and yellow to brown persistent fruit in fall; and dark, deeply furrowed bark that shows up in winter. Zones 6-9.

Selected species and varieties
O. arboreum, sourwood: has gracefully drooping branches bearing leaves that are ovate and 3 to 8 inches long, and flower clusters that are 10 inches long or more.

Growing conditions
Sourwood grows in full sun or partial shade and in moist, well-drained, very acid soil. It needs shelter from winds and does not tolerate urban pollution.

Landscape uses
With its large flower clusters, sourwood makes a spectacular specimen tree. It can also be used as a shade tree, and it grows well as an understory plant among taller trees.

—

Palmetto see *Sabal*

—

Parrotia (par-ROT-ee-a)

Deciduous tree that grows 20 to 40 feet tall. It is low-branched and conical in shape, and may be single- or multiple-stemmed. Zones 5-9.

Selected species and varieties
P. persica, Persian parrotia, Persian witch hazel: leaves are ovate, glossy green in summer and bright yellow, orange and scarlet in fall. Bark is mottled gray, green, white and brown, and it peels year round when the tree is mature.

Growing conditions
Persian witch hazel needs morning sun, shade from other plants in the heat of the afternoon in summer, and protection from winter sun and windburn. It prefers well-drained, loamy, slightly acid soil.

Landscape uses
Persian witch hazel may be used as a specimen, shade, accent or street tree.

—

Paulownia (paw-LOW-nee-a)

Deciduous tree that grows 20 to 60 feet tall and nearly as wide, and bears ornamental flowers in spring and fruit capsules in fall. Zones 6-9.

Selected species and varieties
P. tomentosa, princess tree, empress tree, royal paulownia: grows rapidly into a roundheaded, stiff-branched shade tree 30 to 50 feet tall. Broad, ovate, heart-shaped leaves are 5 to 10 inches long. Vanilla-scented flowers are lilac-colored, with darker spots and yellow stripes inside, and occur in pyramidal clusters 8 to 12 inches long.

Growing conditions
Princess tree grows in full sun or partial shade. Soil must be moist, well drained and deep enough to accommodate the tree's long root system. The tree needs protection from wind, withstands urban pollution and does well in coastal areas.

Landscape uses
Princess tree makes a good specimen or accent tree along a driveway or sidewalk. It provides dense shade that prevents grass from growing beneath it.

—

Pavia see *Aesculus*
Peacock flower see *Delonix*
Pear see *Pyrus*
Pecan see *Carya*

Pepperidge see *Nyssa*

—

Persea (PUR-see-a)

Tropical evergreen that grows 30 to 60 feet tall and produces fruit that may be small and berry-like or large and fleshy. Zones 7-10.

Selected species and varieties
P. borbonia, red bay, swamp red bay, sweet bay, laurel tree, tisswood, Florida mahogany: grows 30 to 40 feet tall. Fruit is dark blue to blackish and borne on red stalks. Leaves are 2 to 8 inches long and pointed at the tips, glossy green in color and fuzzy on the undersides. Zones 8-10.

Growing conditions
Sweet bay requires full sun and moist, average garden soil.

Landscape uses
Sweet bay makes a good specimen or accent tree.

—

Persian witch hazel
see *Parrotia*

Persimmon see *Diospyros*

Petticoat palm
see *Washingtonia*

—

Phellodendron
(fell-o-DEN-dron)
Cork tree

Deciduous tree that grows rapidly 30 to 60 feet tall. It has a short trunk and tortuous branches that give it a sculptured look. Zones 3-7.

Selected species and varieties
P. amurense, Amur cork tree: broad, spreading tree that grows 30 to 45 feet tall. Corky, furrowed bark is gray-brown. Leaves are glossy dark green in summer and yellow briefly in fall. Fleshy black fruit is ½ inch in diameter. Both leaves and fruit give off a scent like turpentine when they are crushed.

Growing conditions
Cork tree needs full sun and will adapt to almost any kind of soil. It is generally trouble-free and maintenance-free.

Landscape uses
Cork tree makes a good specimen or shade tree on areas large enough to accommodate it.

Phoenix (FEE-nicks)
Date palm

Tropical evergreen that grows to 60 feet and has swordlike leaves that arch outward from the top of a straight trunk. Zones 9 and 10.

Selected species and varieties
P. canariensis, Canary Island date palm: has a rough, fibrous trunk composed of lopped-off stem stubs that create a diamond-like bark pattern as the tree ages. At maturity, the trunk reaches 50 feet in height and 3 feet in diameter and the leaves grow 15 to 20 feet long. After 10 to 15 years the tree produces red dates that hang in clusters from long, yellow stalks.

Growing conditions
Date palm must have full sun and fertile soil.

Landscape uses
Date palms make good street trees and can be used to line driveways.

—

Picea (PY-see-a)
Spruce

Evergreen conifer that grows 20 to 100 feet tall in a pyramidal shape with sharp-pointed, spirally arranged needles that are ½ to 1 inch long. Zones 1-7.

Selected species and varieties
P. abies, Norway spruce: grows rapidly, reaching 40 to 80 feet in height and 20 to 30 feet in spread. Needles are lustrous green, branchlets are pendulous and cones are up to 6 inches long. Zones 3-7. 'Cupressiana', Cupress Norway spruce: grows to 50 feet in a narrow, upright form with ascending branches. *P. glauca*, white spruce: similar in appearance to Norway spruce, but its cones are only 1 to 2 inches long and its needles are blue-green with a whitish tinge. Zones 1-5. *P. omorika*, Serbian spruce: grows 60 to 70 feet or more in a graceful, narrow pyramid. Needles are glossy dark green on the upper surface and lined in white on the underside. Cones have fine-toothed scales; they are purplish blue-black when young and mature to reddish brown. Zones 4-8. *P. orientalis*, Oriental spruce: grows 50 to 60 feet. Needles are glossy dark green and only ¼ to ½ inch long. Cones are 2 to 4 inches long; they are reddish

PHELLODENDRON AMURENSE

PHOENIX CANARIENSIS

PICEA ABIES

PICEA PUNGENS 'THOMSEN'

PINUS BUNGEANA

PINUS STROBUS

PINUS THUNBERGIANA

purple when young and turn brown when mature. Zones 5-7. *P. pungens,* Colorado spruce: grows 30 to 75 feet tall with stiff, horizontal branches. Leaves vary in color; they may be green, bluish or silvery white. Cones are 2 to 4 inches long. Zones 2-7. 'Glauca', Colorado blue spruce, grows 30 to 75 feet tall. Needles vary in color from green to silvery blue, and cones are 3½ inches long. Zones 3-7. 'Thomsen' has pale silver-blue foliage.

Growing conditions
Most spruces need full sun and sandy, acid, moist but well-drained soil. White spruce is the hardiest species; it survives winters of −70° F and summers of 110° F. Serbian spruce needs to be protected from cold wind. Oriental spruce is an exception in that it prefers clay soil; it cannot tolerate extremely wet or extremely dry soil, strong winds or polluted air. Colorado spruce prefers cool soil.

Landscape uses
Singly spruces make majestic specimen trees, and in massed plantings they make good screens and windbreaks.

—

Pine see *Pinus*

—

Pinus (PY-nus)
Pine

Diverse genus of evergreen conifers that grow from 10 to more than 100 feet tall. They are generally conical when young and develop rounded tops with age; but of all needle-leaved evergreens, pines have the widest range of characteristics, habit and distribution. Zones 2-9.

Selected species and varieties
P. bungeana, lacebark pine: grows 30 to 50 feet tall, generally in a bushy shape, with multiple trunks and mottled, exfoliating bark. Needles are 4 inches long on gray-green twigs. Cones are 2 to 3 inches long. Zones 5-8. *P. cembra,* Swiss stone pine: grows very slowly to 25 to 40 feet or more with 2- to 3-inch lustrous, dark green needles having white lines. Cones are 2 to 3 inches long. Young stems are covered with orange hair that turns gray-

black as they age. Zones 3-7. *P. contorta,* lodgepole pine: grows 25 to 30 feet tall and has yellowish green needles that are 1½ inches long and twisted. Cones are 1½ inches long. Zones 5-8. 'Contorta', shore pine: has a crooked trunk and twisted branches. 'Latifolia', lodgepole pine: grows taller, 70 to 80 feet, and has longer, broader, lighter green needles.

P. densiflora, Japanese red pine: grows slowly to 50 to 60 feet. It has an irregular crown and a twisted, often leaning, trunk with orange-red bark. Needles are 3 to 5 inches long. Cones are 2 inches long. Zones 3-7. 'Oculus-draconis', dragon's eye pine, has variegated foliage, each needle having two yellow bands. Zones 6 and 7. *P. flexilis,* limber pine: grows slowly to 30 to 50 feet tall. Zones 4-7. Needles are 2½ to 3½ inches long, cones are up to 6 inches long, and branchlets are so supple that they can be twisted for decorations.

P. koraiensis, Korean pine: similar to Swiss stone pine and is hardy enough to grow in Zone 3. *P. nigra,* Austrian pine: grows 50 to 60 feet in height and 20 to 40 feet in spread and has multiple stems. Needles are 4 to 6 inches long with fine-toothed margins. Cones are 2 to 3 inches long and 1 to 1¼ inches wide, and tawny yellow when young. Zones 4-7. *P. palustris,* longleaf pine, Florida pine, Georgia pine: grows 80 to 90 feet tall. Needles are 8 to 18 inches long. Cones are 10 inches long and remain on the tree up to 20 years. Zones 7-10. *P. parviflora,* Japanese white pine: grows to 50 feet or more. Needles are 1½ inches long and are bluish green; cones are 3 inches long. Zones 4-7. 'Glauca' has fine-textured, twisted, whitened, blue-green foliage.

P. resinosa, red pine: grows 50 to 80 feet. Needles are 5 to 6 inches long; bark is orange-red on young trees and turns reddish brown with age. Zones 2-5. *P. strobus,* eastern white pine: grows 50 to 80 feet tall or more. Leaves are 3 to 5 inches long and blue-green. Cones are cylindrical, 6 to 8 inches long and 1⅗ inches wide. Zones 3-8. *P. sylvestris,* Scotch pine: grows 30 to 60 feet tall. Needles are 3 inches long and twisted. Bark is rough and red-orange. Cones are 1½ to 3 inches long. Zones 2-7. *P. thunbergiana,* Japanese black pine:

grows 20 to 40 feet tall and has multiple stems. Needles are dark green, 2½ to 7 inches long, twisted and densely crowded. Zones 6-9.

Growing conditions
Pines need full sun and moist, well-drained soil. Lodgepole pine tolerates wet soil; limber pine tolerates dry soil. Japanese white pine and Japanese black pine tolerate salt. Eastern white pine needs a humid atmosphere. Austrian pine withstands urban pollution.

Landscape uses
All pines can be used singly as specimen trees and in massed plantings for screens. Austrian pine makes a good street tree because of its tolerance for pollution. Japanese black pine is a good tree for the seashore.

Pistache see *Pistacia*

Pistacia (pis-TAY-she-a)
Pistache

Deciduous and evergreen trees that grow 30 to 60 feet tall, have rounded crowns, feather-like leaves, inconspicuous flowers and berry-like fruit. Zones 7-10.

Selected species and varieties
P. chinensis, Chinese pistache: grows rapidly to 30 to 45 feet in height. Leaves are dark green in summer and turn bright red to orange in autumn. Fruit is ¼ inch in diameter; it is red at first and matures to robin's egg blue. Zones 7-9.

Growing conditions
Chinese pistache needs full sun and does best in moist, well-drained soil, but it can tolerate drought.

Landscape uses
Chinese pistache is suited for use as a specimen, accent, shade or street tree.

Plane tree see *Platanus*

Platanus (PLAT-a-nus)
Sycamore, buttonwood, plane tree

Deciduous shade tree that grows 75 to 100 feet in height and spreads as wide. It has a massive trunk and crooked branches. Zones 4-10.

Selected species and varieties
P. × *acerifolia,* London plane tree: similar to sycamore but does not spread quite so wide and bears its fruit in twos and threes. Zones 6-9. *P. occidentalis,* American plane tree, American buttonwood, eastern sycamore, buttonball: leaves are large, 4 to 9 inches wide, with three to five triangular lobes, and coarsely toothed. Fruits occur in tight, spiny, round balls that hang singly from long stalks and often persist through winter. Bark is grayish brown and flakes off to reveal a cream-colored inner bark, giving a mottled appearance. Zones 4-9.

Growing conditions
Plane trees prefer full sun and moist, well-drained soil, but are extremely adaptable and will grow almost anywhere.

Landscape uses
Plane trees make good specimen and shade trees on areas large enough to accommodate them.

Plum see *Prunus*

Podocarpus (po-do-CAR-pus)

Evergreen tree that grows 25 to 100 feet tall in an oval to pyramidal shape and bears fleshy red fruit. Zones 8-10.

Selected species and varieties
P. macrophyllus, yew podocarpus, Buddhist pine, southern yew: columnar tree that grows 25 to 35 feet tall and half as wide. Leaves are ½ to 2¾ inches long, needle-like and spirally arranged on branches. Zones 8-10. *P. nagi,* broadleaf podocarpus, Japanese podocarpus: pyramidal tree that grows 30 to 40 feet tall and has 1- to 3-inch-long oval-shaped leaves on drooping branches. Zones 9 and 10.

Growing conditions
Podocarpus grows in full sun or partial shade. It needs fertile, well-drained soil and protection from winter sun and wind.

Landscape uses
Singly podocarpus makes a good specimen. Several together make good windbreaks.

PISTACIA CHINENSIS

PLATANUS OCCIDENTALIS

PODOCARPUS MACROPHYLLUS

POPULUS TREMULOIDES

PRUNUS SUBHIRTELLA 'PENDULA'

Poinciana see *Delonix*

Poplar see *Populus*

—

Populus (POP-yew-lus)
Poplar

Fast-growing deciduous tree that grows 40 to 100 feet tall. It has dangling catkins that emerge before the leaves. Fruit is usually a small capsule. Bark is gray and furrowed. Zones 1-9.

Selected species and varieties
P. alba, white poplar: grows 40 to 80 feet tall with an irregular, broadly rounded crown. Leaves are dark green, 2 to 5 inches long, three- to five-lobed, and white to silvery and felty on the undersides. They usually fall early in autumn before showing color. Zones 3-8. 'Pyramidalis', bolleana poplar: a tall, narrow, columnar tree that grows 45 to 50 feet tall. It becomes pyramidal in old age. Leaves are shiny white on the undersides. *P. deltoides,* eastern cottonwood: grows 75 to 100 feet in height and 40 to 50 feet in spread. It is pyramidal when young and later becomes vase-shaped. Leaves are bright green and 5 inches long. Zones 2-8. 'Siouxland' is a male form sometimes called cottonless cottonwood because it has no fruit or seeds. *P. nigra,* Lombardy poplar: narrow, columnar tree that grows 30 to 60 feet tall and 1 to 2 feet wide. Zones 3-9. *P. tremuloides,* quaking aspen: grows 40 to 50 feet tall with a 20- to 30-foot spread. It is narrow and pyramidal when young and develops a rounded crown with age. Leaves are 1½ to 3 inches long and wide, dark green in summer and yellow in the fall. Bark is smooth and pale green on young trees, and fissured and dark on mature ones. Zones 1-5.

Growing conditions
Poplar, cottonwood and aspen grow best in full sun and deep, moist, well-drained soil, but they adapt to a wide variety of growing conditions. They tolerate drought, urban pollution and salt spray. Pruning should be done in summer to avoid bleeding.

Landscape uses
Poplars make good screens, windbreaks and property dividers. Because they have invasive roots they serve well for erosion control.

Princess tree see *Paulownia*

—

Prunus (PROO-nus)

Large genus of deciduous flowering fruit trees that includes plum, cherry, peach, apricot and almond. They grow from 15 to 60 feet tall. Zones 2-9.

Selected species and varieties
P. × blireiana, blireiana plum: grows 25 feet tall. It has a rounded, densely branched crown, small purple leaves that fade to green and double 1¼-inch pink flowers. Zones 6-9. *P. campanulata,* bell-flowered cherry, Taiwan cherry: grows 20 to 30 feet tall in an erect form with deep rose ¾-inch flowers. Leaves emerge bright green and turn dark green as they mature. Zones 6-9. *P. cerasifera,* cherry plum: rounded tree that grows to 25 feet with spreading branches. Flowers are white; fruit is 1 inch in diameter and may be yellow or reddish. 'Atropurpurea' has narrow-leaved, reddish purple foliage that tends to fade, and light pink flowers. Zones 5-9. 'Thundercloud' is similar to 'Atropurpurea', but it holds its purple leaf color throughout the season. Zones 6-9. *P. × incam* 'Okame', Okame cherry: grows 20 to 30 feet tall. It has reddish pink flowers that last for two to three weeks, longer than many other cherries. Leaves turn yellow, orange and red in fall. Zones 5-8. *P. maackii,* Amur chokecherry: 35- to 45-foot roundheaded, densely branched ornamental with coppery brown bark that peels in thin, curly strips. Small, white flowers bloom profusely in May and are followed by small, black fruit. Foliage emerges early in spring and falls early in autumn. Zones 2-6. *P. sargentii,* Sargent cherry: upright, rounded tree that grows to 40 to 50 feet tall with saw-toothed, 3- to 5-inch leaves; they are dark green in summer and turn red to bronze in fall. Bark is glossy and red to chestnut brown. Pink flowers are followed by purplish black fruit that ripens in June and July. Zones 4-7. *P. serotina,* black cherry: grows 50 to 60 feet with an oval crown and pendulous branches. Leaves are dark green in summer and turn yellow to red in fall. Flowers are white. Fruits emerge red; in August they ripen to black and are edi-

ble. Zones 4-9. *P. serrula,* paper-bark cherry: grows up to 30 feet tall and has shiny mahogany-colored bark that peels. Zones 6-8. *P. serrulata,* Japanese flowering cherry: vase-shaped tree that grows to 50 to 75 feet tall. Flowers are ½ to 2½ inches in diameter and range from single to double, white to pinks. Leaves turn bronze in fall. Zones 6-8. 'Amanogawa' is a narrow variety with semidouble fragrant pink flowers and small black fruit. 'Kwanzan' grows to 40 feet and produces an abundance of 2½-inch deep-pink flowers. 'Shirotae', also designated 'Mt. Fuji', has a spreading habit with 2-inch fragrant, white flowers. *P. subhirtella,* Higan cherry: grows 20 to 30 feet tall and half as wide in a weeping form. Flowers are ½ inch in diameter. Fruits are ⅓ inch in diameter and shiny black. Zones 4-8. 'Autumnalis' has a forked trunk, and slender stems with pink flowers that sometimes bloom in fall as well as in the spring. 'Pendula', weeping Higan cherry: has graceful, drooping branches. Zones 6-8. *P.* × *yedoensis,* Yoshino cherry: grows up to 40 feet in a spreading, rounded form and produces fragrant 1-inch flowers that open pink and change to white. Zones 5-8.

Growing conditions
Most cherries will flourish in full sun or partial shade, except purple leaf cultivars, which need full sun to bring out their color. Cherry plums adapt to any good, well-drained soil. Chokecherries require sandy, well-drained soil.

Landscape uses
Cherry plums make good specimen, accent and patio trees. The tall species provide shade.

Pseudolarix
(soo-do-LAIR-iks)
Golden larch

Deciduous conifer that grows slowly to 30 to 50 feet. It is related to the pine family. Zones 6 and 7.

Selected species and varieties
P. kaempferi: broad, pyramidal tree with spreading branches and gracefully descending side branchlets. Flat, needle-like leaves are light green until fall, when they turn yellow and drop. Cones are golden brown and fleshy. Zones 5-7.

Growing conditions
Golden larch prefers full sun and moist, acid, well-drained, deep soil. In Zone 5 it needs to be protected from wind.

Landscape uses
Golden larches make good specimen trees and screens.

Pseudotsuga (soo-doe-SOO-ga)

Evergreen conifer that grows up to 100 feet tall in a conical to pyramidal shape. It is related to the pine family. Zones 3-7.

Selected species and varieties
P. menziesii, Douglas fir: grows 40 to 60 feet tall. It is pyramidal in shape and has wide-spreading branches; the upper branches ascend and the lower branches descend. Needles are 1 to 1½ inches long and blunt; they are dark green on the upper sides and banded in white on the undersides. Cones are oval-shaped and 2 to 4 inches long; they are purplish when young and turn yellow-brown when they mature. Zones 4-6. *P. menziesii glauca,* Rocky Mountain Douglas fir: slower growing, more compact variety with bluish green needles. Zones 4-7.

Growing conditions
Douglas fir needs full sun, a humid climate and moist, well-drained acid to neutral soil. It should have protection from winds because its roots are shallow and it can easily be uprooted.

Landscape uses
Singly Douglas fir makes a spectacular specimen tree; several together make a good windbreak.

Pterostyrax (tear-o-STY-racks)
Epaulette tree

Deciduous tree that grows 20 to 50 feet tall. It has toothed leaves and white flowers in sprays. Zones 5-8.

Selected species and varieties
P. hispidus, fragrant epaulette tree: slender-branched, spreading tree. Fragrant, white flowers bloom in 9- to 10-inch-long pendulous sprays after the leaves are fully open. Leaves are 3 to 7½ inches long, bright green on top and silvery green underneath.

PSEUDOLARIX KAEMPFERI

PSEUDOTSUGA MENZIESII

PTEROSTYRAX HISPIDUS

PYRUS CALLERYANA 'BRADFORD'

QUERCUS VIRGINIANA

Growing conditions

Epaulette tree needs full sun and moist, sandy loam. It should have protection from strong winds and winter cold.

Landscape uses

Epaulette tree makes a good specimen tree for a small yard or patio.

—

Pyrus (PY-rus)
Pear

Deciduous and semievergreen trees, 20 to 60 feet tall, grown for their ornamental white flowers. Zones 4-10.

Selected species and varieties

P. calleryana, Callery pear: has an open, oval to conical crown that is 15 to 30 feet in spread. Leaves have scalloped edges; they are glossy dark green in summer and turn crimson red in autumn. 'Aristocrat' has attractive leathery leaves that turn yellow to red in autumn. 'Bradford' grows 30 to 50 feet. It has a compact pyramidal crown and cloudlike cover of flowers in early spring. Leaves turn scarlet or purple in autumn. Zones 5-8. 'Capital' has an upright habit and leaves that turn coppery brown in autumn. 'Red Spire' is pyramidal in form and has leaves that turn yellow in fall. *P. kawakamii,* evergreen pear: grows in an irregular shape to 30 feet tall. Flowers appear on the tree from late winter through spring. Zones 8-10. *P. salicifolia,* willowleaf pear: grows 15 to 25 feet tall and has silvery, willow-like leaves. Zones 4-7. 'Pendula' has drooping branches.

Growing conditions

Pear trees prefer full sun but are easy to grow and adapt to nearly all soils. They can withstand air pollution, drought and wind.

Landscape uses

Pear trees make good street and shade trees. Small species can be container-grown for use on patios.

—

Quaking aspen see *Populus*

—

Quercus (KWER-kus)
Oak

Deciduous and broad-leaved evergreen trees, 35 to 100 feet tall, that are distributed across the North American continent in both cold and tropical regions. Zones 2-10.

Selected species and varieties

Q. acutissima, sawtooth oak: grows 35 to 45 feet tall. It is pyramidal when young and ages to a broadly rounded, spreading form. Leaves are 3½ to 7½ inches long, 1 to 2¼ inches wide; they emerge yellow in spring, turn dark green in summer and change to yellow or golden brown in fall. Acorns are 1 inch long. Zones 6-9. *Q. agrifolia,* California live oak: evergreen that grows to 50 feet. It has a rounded crown, broadly spreading branches, shiny, spine-tipped green leaves and dark gray to black bark. Acorns are pointed. Zones 9 and 10. *Q. alba,* white oak: grows to 75 feet in an erect form. It has wide-spreading branches and round-lobed leaves that turn wine to crimson in fall. Acorns are ½ to ¾ inches long with rounded ends. Bark is light gray and shallowly fissured. Zones 3-9. *Q. bicolor,* swamp white oak: deciduous tree that grows 50 to 60 feet tall and has a broad, round crown. Six-inch-long leaves are coarsely toothed, shiny green on the upper surfaces and felty white on the undersides. Bark is grayish brown, vertically fissured and flaky. Zones 4-8. *Q. coccinea,* scarlet oak: grows to 75 feet. Deeply lobed leaves turn scarlet in fall. Zones 5-9. *Q. imbricaria,* shingle oak: grows 50 to 60 feet in height and width. Leaves are 2½ to 6 inches long, shiny and unlobed, and turn russet in fall. Zones 5-8. *Q. macrocarpa,* bur oak, mossy cup oak: deciduous tree that grows 70 to 90 feet tall. Leaves are 4 to 10 inches long, rounded on the tips and yellow in fall. Acorns are up to 1½ inches long. Bark is dark gray, thick and deeply furrowed. Zones 2-8. *Q. myrsinifolia,* Chinese evergreen oak: compact, roundheaded tree that grows to 30 feet. Leaves are narrowly ovate, 2 to 4½ inches long, ¾ to 1¼ inches wide and pointed at the tip. Zones 7-9. *Q. palustris,* pin oak: grows 60 to 75 feet tall in a pyramidal shape. The lower branches are pendulous, and the upper ones are upright; mature trees lose their lower branches. Leaves are 3 to 6 inches long and have five to seven lobes with deep U-shaped indentations between the lobes. They turn soft tan in fall. Acorns are ½ inch in diameter and globe-shaped. Zones 4-8. *Q. phellos,* willow oak: grows up to 60 feet tall and wide. It is pyramidal in youth and develops a rounded form as it ages. Leaves are 2 to 5½ inches long and only ½ inch wide; they turn yellowish brown to russet red in fall. Acorns are ½ inch long and rounded. Zones 6-9. *Q. robur,* English oak, truffle oak: deciduous tree that grows 75 to 100 feet tall and wide. It has a rounded crown and a short trunk. Leaves are 2 to 5 inches long and ¾ to 2½ inches wide and have rounded lobes. Zones 5-9. 'Fastigiata' grows 50 to 60 feet tall in a narrow, columnar form. *Q. rubra,* red oak: grows 60 to 80 feet in height, 40 to 50 feet in spread, and has a round crown. Leaves are 4½ to 8½ inches long, 4 to 6 inches wide and sometimes have as many as 11 lobes. They emerge pink to red in spring, turn dark green in summer and change to bright red in fall. Zones 3-9. *Q. virginiana,* southern live oak: evergreen tree that grows 40 to 80 feet in height, 60 to 100 feet in spread. Branches are contorted. Leaves are elliptic, 1¼ to 3 inches long and ⅜ to 1 inch wide. They are dark green and leathery on the upper surfaces, gray-green and woolly on the undersides. Zones 8-10.

Growing conditions
Nearly all oaks need full sun and moist, acid, well-drained, rich, deep soil. Swamp white oak and pin oak prefer wet soil. Only shingle oak tolerates dry soil.

Landscape uses
Oaks make majestic specimens and cast deep shade. They may be used as street trees. Fastigiate English oak can provide a vertical accent.

—

Quince see *Cydonia*

Red bay see *Persea*

Redbud see *Cercis*

Red cedar see *Juniperus*

—

Robinia (ro-BIN-ee-a)
Locust

Deciduous shade tree that grows 25 to 80 feet tall. It has feather-like leaves, stems that may be armed with spines, clusters of pea-shaped flowers, and dry pods. Zones 3-8.

Selected species and varieties
R. pseudoacacia, black locust: grows 50 to 75 feet tall with upright branches and a slender, oblong crown. Fragrant, white flowers appear from May to early June. Leaves consist of six to 19 rounded leaflets. Pods are 2 to 4 inches long, smooth and brownish black. Zones 4-8.

Growing conditions
Black locust needs full sun but thrives in poor soil.

Landscape uses
Black locust is a good tree for difficult terrain; it has tenacious roots that will take hold on a steep slope and prevent soil erosion.

—

Royal palm see *Roystonea*

—

Roystonea (roy-STO-nee-a)
Royal palm

Tropical evergreen tree that grows 50 to 100 feet tall with a manelike crown of arching fronds. Zone 10.

Selected species and varieties
R. regis, royal palm: grows to a height of 60 feet or more. It has a long, unbranched trunk from which a fountain-like spray of 8- to 10-foot-long fronds emerges at the apex. The bark is smooth, gray and ringed.

Growing conditions
Royal palm grows in full sun or partial shade and in moist loam or clay soil.

Landscape uses
Royal palm makes a good specimen or street tree.

—

Russian olive see *Elaeagnus*

—

Sabal (SAY-bal)
Palmetto

Tropical evergreen that grows 10 to 100 feet tall. It has a round, compact crown of fan-shaped leaves that split into ribbon-like sections as they mature. Zones 8-10.

Selected species and varieties
S. palmetto, cabbage palm: trunk is stout and covered with sheaths of dried leaves that form a crisscross

ROBINIA PSEUDOACACIA

ROYSTONEA REGIS

SABAL PALMETTO

SALIX BABYLONICA

SAPINDUS DRUMMONDII

SAPIUM SEBIFERUM

pattern. White or pale yellow flowers appear in summer and are followed by ½-inch black fruits.

Growing conditions
Cabbage palm grows in full sun or partial shade, and in moist or dry soil.

Landscape uses
Singly cabbage palm makes a good accent; several together can be planted in a border.

Salix (SAY-liks)
Willow

Deciduous tree that grows 15 to 75 feet tall with arched branches that sweep the ground. Leaves are long and narrow. Small flowers are borne in dense catkins. Zones 2-9.

Selected species and varieties
S. alba 'Trista', golden weeping willow: grows 50 to 75 feet tall and wide. It has pendulous golden twigs and narrow leaves. Zones 2-8. *S. babylonica*, Babylon weeping willow: grows 30 to 40 feet on a short, stout trunk and has a rounded crown. Leaves emerge pale green in spring and turn dull green in summer and yellow in autumn. Light green catkins appear among the leaves in spring. Zones 7-9. *S. matsudana* 'Tortuosa', corkscrew willow: grows 30 to 50 feet tall. Unlike most willows, it has branches that ascend rather than droop. Twigs occur in twisted spirals. Zones 5-9.

Growing conditions
Willows grow in full sun or partial shade and need wet soil.

Landscape uses
Willows make good specimens and accent trees. They are especially suited to planting alongside rivers and lakes.

Sapindus (sap-IND-us)
Soapberry

Evergreen and deciduous trees that grow 30 to 60 feet tall. They produce berry-like fruit that lathers and was used for washing by the American Indians. Zones 6-10.

Selected species and varieties
S. drummondii: deciduous tree that grows 25 to 50 feet tall and spreads nearly as wide. It has an upright, rounded crown. Leaves

are feather-like and have four to nine pairs of sickle-shaped leaflets. They are glossy on the upper surfaces and fuzzy on the undersides, green in spring and summer, and yellow in fall. Bark is scaly and reddish brown. Yellow-white flowers emerge in spring in 6- to 10-inch sprays. Fruit is ½ inch in diameter, yellow-orange when it ripens in October; it persists through winter and eventually turns black.

Growing conditions
Soapberry grows in full sun or light shade and in soil that is sandy, dry or rocky.

Landscape uses
Soapberry makes a good specimen, shade tree or street tree.

Sapium (SAY-pi-um)

Deciduous tree that grows 30 to 40 feet tall. Zones 8-10.

Selected species and varieties
S. sebiferum, Chinese tallow tree: deciduous tree that grows in a graceful form with a rounded, stately crown. Flowers are yellowish green and are followed by brown capsules that open to expose waxy, white fruit. Branchlets exude a poisonous milky juice when bruised. Leaves are 1½ to 3 inches long and broad with pointed tips; they turn yellow, orange or red in fall.

Growing conditions
Chinese tallow tree needs full sun and grows in most dry soils. It tolerates drought.

Landscape uses
Chinese tallow tree makes a good specimen tree for a patio. Because it grows rapidly, it can provide quick shade.

Sassafras (SAS-a-fras)

Deciduous tree that grows up to 60 feet tall. It is noted for its aromatic bark, roots, branches, leaves, flowers and fruit. Zones 5-9.

Selected species and varieties
S. albidum: grows 30 to 60 feet in an irregular shape with horizontal, contorted branching. Leaves are sometimes mitten-shaped, sometimes three-lobed, sometimes unlobed; all shapes may appear on the same tree at the same time. They

turn shades of orange and red in fall. Bark is reddish brown and furrowed. Flowers are yellowish green and bloom in spring. Fruits are fleshy and blue, and appear on red stalks.

Growing conditions
Sassafras grows in full sun or partial shade. It prefers moist, loamy, acid, well-drained soil and needs protection from wind.

Landscape uses
Sassafras makes a good specimen or shade tree. Several together can be used in a woodsy border.

—

Sciadopitys (sy-a-DOP-it-is)

Pyramidal evergreen conifer that grows 20 to 40 feet tall with branches that rise upward at the tips. Zones 5-8.

Selected species and varieties
S. verticillata, Japanese umbrella tree: has branches that are horizontal when young and become pendulous with age. Leaves may be spirally arranged, scalelike and crowded near the branchlet tips, or linear, flat and whorled in clusters of 20 to 30. Cones are 2 to 4 inches long and take two years to mature.

Growing conditions
Japanese umbrella tree grows in full sun or shade and in moist, well-drained acid soil. It needs protection from wind.

Landscape uses
Japanese umbrella tree makes a good specimen or accent. Several together can be planted in a border.

—

Senna see *Cassia*

Serviceberry see *Amelanchier*

Shadbush see *Amelanchier*

She-oak see *Casuarina*

Shower tree see *Cassia*

Silk tree see *Albizia*

Silver bell see *Halesia*

Silver dollar tree
see *Eucalyptus*

Smoke tree see *Cotinus*

Snowbell see *Styrax*

Snowdrop tree see *Halesia*

Soapberry see *Sapindus*

Sophora (so-FO-ra)

Deciduous and evergreen trees that grow 20 to 75 feet tall with rounded crowns, showy flowers and beanlike seeds. Zones 5-8.

Selected species and varieties
S. japonica 'Regent', Japanese pagoda tree, Chinese scholar tree: deciduous tree that grows 20 to 60 feet tall. Flowers are slightly fragrant, ½ inch long and creamy white, and appear in 15-inch-long sprays in summer. Seedpods are 2 to 4 inches long and greenish yellow; they ripen in October and persist through winter. Leaves are 6 to 10 inches long and have seven to 17 leaflets. *S. secundiflora,* mescal bean, frijolito: broad-leaved evergreen tree that grows up to 35 feet tall. Flowers are 1 inch long and violet-blue. Pods are up to 8 inches long and emit red seeds.

Growing conditions
Sophoras need full sun and fertile, well-drained soil. Once established they can tolerate heat, drought and air pollution.

Landscape uses
Sophoras can be used for specimens, accents, shade trees and street trees.

—

Sorbus (SORE-bus)
Mountain ash

Deciduous tree that grows 20 to 50 feet tall and is known for its showy spring flowers and its autumn berry clusters. Zones 3-7.

Selected species and varieties
S. alnifolia, Korean mountain ash: grows 40 to 50 feet tall. It has a rounded crown and 2- to 4-inch leaves that turn orange to red in fall. Flowers are white, ¾ inches in diameter, and bloom in flat-topped clusters in May. Fruit is orange to red and ¼ inch in diameter. Bark is smooth and silvery gray. Zones 4-7. *S. aucuparia,* European mountain ash: grows 20 to 40 feet tall. It has an oval crown and leaves composed of nine to 15 toothed leaflets. Zones 3-6.

Growing conditions
Mountain ash does best in full sun and in well-drained soil.

Landscape uses
Mountain ash makes a good specimen or shade tree.

SASSAFRAS ALBIDUM

SCIADOPITYS VERTICILLATA

SOPHORA JAPONICA 'REGENT'

SORBUS ALNIFOLIA

SPHAEROPTERIS COOPERI

STEWARTIA PSEUDOCAMELLIA

STYRAX OBASSIA

SYRINGA RETICULATA

Sorrel tree see *Oxydendrum*

Sour gum see *Nyssa*

Sourwood see *Oxydendrum*

Southern magnolia
see *Magnolia*

Southern yew see *Podocarpus*

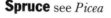

Sphaeropteris
(sfe-ROP-ter-is)
Tree fern

Tropical evergreen tree that has a crown of finely cut fronds cascading from atop 18- to 50-foot trunks. Zones 9 and 10.

Selected species and varieties
S. cooperi, sometimes designated *Alsophila cooperi*, Australian tree fern: grows up to 20 feet tall with a fibrous trunk and 10-foot fronds.

Growing conditions
Australian tree fern prefers partial shade. It needs rich, moist soil and high humidity.

Landscape uses
Australian tree fern can be container-grown for use on a patio.

Spruce see *Picea*

Stewartia (stew-ART-ee-a)

Deciduous tree that grows slowly to 20 to 40 feet tall in a pyramidal shape. It has waxy white flowers that bloom in summer and flaking bark that gives it a mottled appearance. Zones 5-8.

Selected species and varieties
S. koreana, Korean stewartia: grows 20 to 25 feet tall with branches that zigzag. Flowers are 3 inches in diameter. Leaves are oval, 2 to 4 inches long, ¾ to 3 inches wide and toothed; they turn orange-red in fall. Bark is mottled grayish brown and orange-brown. Zones 6 and 7. *S. pseudocamellia*, Japanese stewartia: grows to 30 to 40 feet tall. Leaves are 1½ to 3½ inches long and turn yellow, red or purplish red in fall.

Growing conditions
Stewartias need partial shade from hot afternoon sun. They grow best in moist, loamy acid soil. Once planted, they should not be moved.

Landscape uses
Stewartias make good specimen and accent trees.

Styrax (STY-raks)
Snowbell

Deciduous tree that grows 20 to 30 feet tall and bears showy white flowers. Zones 5-9.

Selected species and varieties
S. japonicus, Japanese snowbell: has horizontal branches and pendulous clusters of fragrant, bell-shaped flowers. Leaves are 1 to 3½ inches long and often turn yellow in autumn. The bark is dark gray and smooth. Zones 6-8. *S. obassia*, fragrant snowbell: similar to Japanese snowbell, but has 8-inch-long leaves and upright branches. Zones 5-8.

Growing conditions
Snowbell grows in sun or shade and does best in moist, well-drained, acid soil.

Landscape uses
Snowbell may be used as a specimen, on a patio or in a border.

Sweet bay see *Laurus*

Sweet gum see *Liquidamber*

Sweet olive see *Osmanthus*

Sycamore see *Platanus*

Syringa (sy-RING-a)
Lilac

Deciduous tree that grows 20 to 30 feet tall and wide. It has showy flowers that may be white, lilac, pink, red or purple. Zones 2-7.

Selected species and varieties
S. reticulata, Japanese tree lilac: has spreading branches and reddish brown bark. Flowers are white and fragrant, and appear in 6- to 12-inch-long clusters in summer after other lilacs have faded. Leaves are heart-shaped, 2 to 7 inches long. Zones 3-7. 'Ivory Silk' grows 20 feet in a compact oval shape.

Growing conditions
Japanese tree lilac needs full sun and loose, slightly acid, well-drained soil. It should be pruned after it has flowered.

Landscape uses

Japanese tree lilac makes a good specimen, accent or street tree.

Taxodium (tax-O-dee-um)
Cypress

Genus of deciduous and evergreen conifers that grow 50 to 80 feet tall in a conical or columnar shape. Trunks are fluted and flared at the base. Zones 5-9.

Selected species and varieties

T. ascendens, pond cypress, pond bald cypress: deciduous tree that grows 70 to 80 feet tall. Leaves are awl-shaped and up to ½ inch long. Cones are purple when young; they are up to 1¼ inches in diameter and may be round or ovoid. Zones 6-9. *T. distichum,* bald cypress: deciduous tree that grows 50 to 70 feet tall with graceful, horizontal branches. Foliage is fine-textured and needle-like, up to ¾ inch long; it is delicate green in spring and summer, and bronze in fall. Bark is reddish brown and fissured.

Growing conditions

Cypresses grow in full sun or partial shade. They are among the few trees that can live with permanently wet roots; they often grow in swampy areas. They will adapt to soil, but the soil must be acid, sandy and moist.

Landscape uses

Pond cypress makes a good vertical accent. Bald cypress may be used as a specimen tree or in a woodsy border.

Taxus (TAX-us)
Yew

Evergreen trees that grow 10 to 60 feet tall. They have needle-like leaves and fleshy, bright-colored fruit. Zones 4-7.

Selected species and varieties

T. baccata, English yew: grows 35 to 60 feet tall and 15 to 25 feet wide. Leaves are ¼ inch long, dark green and shiny on the upper sides, and paler on the undersides. Fruit is red. Zones 6 and 7. *T. cuspidata,* Japanese yew: grows 10 to 40 feet tall and wide. Branches may be spreading or upright. Inch-long leaves are dull green on the upper surfaces and have yellow bands on the undersides. Zones 4-7.

Growing conditions

Yews grow in full sun or partial shade and need moist, fertile, well-drained soil.

Landscape uses

Yews make good specimens, foundation plants, hedges and screens.

Thuja (THOO-ya)
Arborvitae

Genus of evergreen conifers that grow up to 70 feet tall. They have flattened branchlets with soft needle-like leaves and small cones. Zones 2-9.

Selected species and varieties

T. occidentalis, American arborvitae, eastern white cedar: narrow 40- to 60-foot columnar tree having dense, compact, aromatic foliage that is yellow-green to bright green. Bark is reddish brown, fibrous and shreddy. Cones are ½ inch long. Zones 3-7. 'Lutea' grows 30 to 35 feet tall in a pyramidal shape and has bright yellow foliage. Zones 4-7. 'Nigra' has a pyramidal shape and dark green foliage. Zone 4. 'Spiralis' grows 30 to 45 feet tall in a narrow pyramidal form. Leaves are dark green and branches are spiral-shaped. 'Techny' is also a pyramidal form and has dark green foliage. Zones 3-7. *T. orientalis,* sometimes designated *Pladycladus orientalis,* Oriental arborvitae: grows 18 to 25 feet in height and 10 to 12 feet in width. It may be conical or pyramidal; it is compact in youth and becomes open with age. Leaves are bright green to yellow when the tree is young and darken as the tree matures. Cones are ½ to ¾ inch long. Zones 5-9. 'Semperaurescens' has shoots that emerge golden yellow in spring and turn bronze in winter. *T. plicata,* western arborvitae, western white cedar: grows 50 to 70 feet in height and 15 to 25 feet in width. It is pyramidal in shape and has glossy green foliage. Cones are ½ inch long. Zones 5-7.

Growing conditions

All arborvitaes need full sun. Most will adapt to any average, well-drained soil, but eastern and western arborvitaes need deep, moist, well-drained soil and high humidity. They are vulnerable to snow and ice damage and need protection from winter sun scorch.

TAXODIUM ASCENDENS

TAXUS BACCATA

THUJA OCCIDENTALIS

THUJA PLICATA

TILIA CORDATA

TSUGA CANADENSIS

TSUGA CAROLINIANA

ULMUS AMERICANA

Landscape uses

Arborvitaes are suitable for use as accents, hedges, screens and foundation plants.

—

Tilia (TILL-ee-a)
Linden, basswood, limetree

Deciduous shade tree that grows 50 to 80 feet tall with a straight trunk and narrow crown. Flowers are fragrant, leaves are heart-shaped and branchlets zigzag. Zones 2-8.

Selected species and varieties

T. americana, American linden, basswood: fast-growing tree, 60 to 80 feet tall, with a rounded crown. Toothed leaves are 4 to 8 inches long and nearly as wide. Yellow flowers occur in 2- to 3-inch-wide clusters in early summer. *T. cordata,* littleleaf linden: grows slowly to 60 to 70 feet. Three-inch-long leaves have hairy undersides. Zones 3-8. 'Greenspire' has a pear-shaped crown. Zones 4-8. *T.* × *echlora* 'Redmond', Redmond linden: has a pyramidal crown, and reddish buds and twigs in winter. Zones 4-8. *T. tomentosa,* silver linden: 50 to 70 feet tall. White hairs on the leaf undersides, stems and buds give the tree a silvery appearance. Zones 4-7.

Growing conditions

Linden needs full sun and moist, well-drained soil. It cannot tolerate urban pollution.

Landscape uses

Linden makes a good specimen and shade tree.

—

Tisswood see *Persea*

Tree fern see *Sphaeropteris*

Tree-of-heaven see *Ailanthus*

—

Tsuga (TSOO-ga)
Hemlock

Needle-leaved evergreen conifer that grows 30 to 70 feet tall. It has slender leading shoots and irregular horizontal to drooping branches that nod in the breeze. Zones 3-7.

Selected species and varieties

T. canadensis, Canada hemlock: broadly pyramidal tree with a forked trunk that grows 40 to 70

feet tall. Needles are ¼ to ⅔ inch long, rich green on the upper surfaces and banded in white on the undersides. Cones are ½ to 1 inch long. 'Albospicata' is compact and conical. Branch tips are white or variegated. 'Westonigra' has very dark foliage, which shows up best in winter. *T. caroliniana,* Carolina hemlock: grows 40 to 60 feet with dark green needles that radiate around the stems. Cones are 1 to 1½ inches long. Zones 5-7. *T. diversifolia,* Japanese hemlock: compact tree that grows slowly; it seldom exceeds 35 feet tall but may reach 60 feet over a long period. Needles are ½ inch long and radiate from the stem in all directions, showing off white-banded undersides. Zones 5-7.

Growing conditions

Hemlock prefers partial shade; moist, well-drained soil; and a cool and humid climate. It needs shelter from winds and cannot tolerate air pollution.

Landscape uses

Singly hemlock makes a graceful specimen tree; several together make good hedges, screens, windbreaks and background plantings.

—

Tulip tree see *Liriodendron*

Tupelo see *Nyssa*

—

Ulmus (UL-mus)
Elm

Mainly deciduous tree that grows 40 to 90 feet tall. Generally vase-shaped, it has gray, furrowed bark and saw-toothed leaves. Zones 2-9.

Selected species and varieties

U. americana, American elm: grows 60 to 80 feet tall with a spreading crown. Leaves are 3 to 6 inches long, shiny dark green in summer and yellow in fall. *U. carpinifolia,* smooth-leaved elm: grows 70 to 90 feet tall with a pyramidal crown. Leaves are 1½ to 4 inches long and glossy dark green. Zones 4-7. *U. parvifolia,* Chinese elm, lacebark elm: reaches 50 feet. It has a forked trunk, arching branches and mottled, flaking bark. Leaves are ¾ to 2½ inches long, leathery and may turn yellow or reddish purple in fall. Zones 5-9.

'Drake' and 'Sempervirens' have pendulous branches. They may be evergreen in warm regions. Zone 9. 'True Green' tends to be evergreen. Zones 7-9.

Growing conditions
Elm needs full sun and moist, deep, well-drained soil.

Landscape uses
Elm makes a good specimen tree and provides deep shade.

Viburnum (vi-BUR-num)

Genus of evergreen and deciduous trees that reach 30 feet. They have white or pink flowers in spring; in fall they have fleshy ornamental fruits that may be yellow, orange, red, pink, blue or black. Zones 2-9.

Selected species and varieties
V. plicatum: grows to 10 feet with horizontally spreading branches and clusters of white flowers. Leaves are ovate, toothed and 4 inches long. Red fruit turns black in summer. Leaves turn reddish purple in fall. Zones 5-8. *V. prunifolium,* blackhaw viburnum: deciduous tree that grows up to 15 feet tall with a rounded crown. Flowers are white and appear in clusters. Zones 3-9.

Growing conditions
Viburnum grows in sun or shade and in almost any soil.

Landscape uses
Viburnum makes a good specimen tree; several may be massed together for a screen or a border.

Walnut see *Juglans*

Washington fan palm see *Washingtonia*

Washingtonia
(wash-ing-TO-ni-a)
Washington fan palm

Tropical evergreen that grows 30 to 80 feet tall with a long trunk and rounded crown. Zones 9 and 10.

Selected species and varieties
W. filifera, desert fan palm, petticoat palm: grows 50 to 70 feet tall. The trunk is usually obscured by a thick skirt of withered leaves. The crown has light green, segmented leaves that form a fan up to 6 feet

wide. Fibrous threads hang in the leaf margins. In summer, fragrant flowers bloom in clusters along 9-foot branches. Fruit is berry-like, ¼ inch in diameter, black, and it ripens in autumn. *W. robusta,* Mexican fan palm: resembles the desert fan palm but grows up to 90 feet tall and has a narrower shape. Zone 10.

Growing conditions
Washington fan palm needs full sun and moist soil.

Landscape uses
Washington fan palm makes a good specimen tree.

Wattle see *Acacia*

Weeping willow see *Salix*

White cedar see *Chamaecyparis; Thuja*

Whitewood see *Liriodendron*

Willow see *Salix*

Yaupon see *Ilex*

Yellow poplar see *Liriodendron*

Yellowwood see *Cladrastis*

Yew see *Taxus*

Zelkova (zel-KO-va)

Deciduous tree that grows 50 to 80 feet tall, with multiple stems and a vase-shaped crown. Leaves are oval, up to 5 inches long and toothed. Zelkova is often substituted for the American elm because it is resistant to Dutch elm disease. Zones 5-9.

Selected species and varieties
Z. serrata, Japanese zelkova: leaves change from green to yellow or russet in autumn. Bark exfoliates to reveal orange undertones. 'Green Vase' grows rapidly, as much as 3 feet a year, and has upright branches. 'Village Green' also grows rapidly and eventually reaches 60 feet in height. It develops a smooth, straight trunk and has leaves that turn wine red in fall.

Growing conditions
Zelkova needs full sun and deep, moist, well-drained soil. Young trees need protection from frost.

Landscape uses
Zelkova makes a good specimen tree and provides deep shade.

VIBURNUM PLICATUM

WASHINGTONIA FILIFERA

ZELKOVA SERRATA

PICTURE CREDITS

The sources for the illustrations in this book are listed below. Cover photograph by Michael Dirr. Watercolor paintings by Nicholas Fasciano except pages 90, 91, 92, 93, 94, 95: Lorraine Moseley Epstein. Maps on pages 84, 85, 87, 89: digitized by Richard Furno, inked by John Drummond.

Frontispiece paintings listed by page number: 6: *The Garden of the Poets* by Vincent van Gogh, 1888. Courtesy Mr. and Mrs. Lewis Larned Coburn Memorial Collection, © 1988 The Art Institute of Chicago. All rights reserved. 28: *The Blooming Almond Tree* by Pierre Bonnard, 1946. Courtesy Photographic Service of the National Museum of Modern Art, National Museum of Art and Culture, Pompidou Center, Paris. © ARS N.Y./ADAGP/SPADEM, 1988. 42: *Trees* by Sotatsu, early-17th-century Japanese folding screen. (62.30) Courtesy of the Freer Gallery of Art, Smithsonian Institution, Washington, D.C. 54: *Autumn Foliage with Two Youths Fishing* by Winslow Homer. Bequest of Mrs. S. McCormick, courtesy Museum of Fine Arts, Boston.

Photographs in Chapters 1 through 4 from the following sources, listed by page number: 8, 12, 14, 16, 22, 24: Horticultural Photography, Corvallis, OR. 30, 34: Bob Grant. 36: Horticultural Photography, Corvallis, OR. 38, 40: Bob Grant. 44: Horticultural Photography, Corvallis, OR. 46: Pamela Harper. 48, 50, 52: Horticultural Photography, Corvallis, OR. 56, 57: Steven Still. 60: Horticultural Photography, Corvallis, OR. 64: Bob Grant. 66: Pamela Zilly. 70, 74: Horticultural Photography, Corvallis, OR. 78: Michael Dirr.

Photographs in the Dictionary of Trees from the following sources, listed by page and numbered from top to bottom. Details in the dictionary designated as A. Page 98, 1, 1A: Paul Kingsley; 2, 2A: Horticultural Photography, Corvallis, OR.; 3, 3A: Michael Dirr. 99, 1, 1A, 2, 2A, 3A: Pamela Harper; 3: Michael Dirr. 100, 1, 1A: Horticultural Photography, Corvallis, OR.; 2, 2A: Michael Dirr.; 3: Al Bussewitz/Photo-Nats.; 3A: Marilyn Wood/Photo-Nats. 101, 1: Pamela Harper; 1A: Horticultural Photography, Corvallis, OR.; 2, 2A: Bob Grant. 3, 3A: Pamela Harper; 4, 4A: Al Bussewitz/Photo-Nats. 102, 1: Horticultural Photography, Corvallis, OR.; 1A: Pamela Harper; 2, 2A: Horticultural Photography, Corvallis, OR.; 3, 3A: William Aplin. 103, 1, 1A, 2, 2A: Pamela Harper. 104, 1: Horticultural Photography, Corvallis, OR.; 1A: Pamela Harper; 2, 2A: Darrel Apps; 3: Pamela Harper; 3A: Steven Still; 4, 4A: Horticultural Photography, Corvallis, OR. 105, 1, 1A: Michael Dirr; 2: Runk/Schoenberger from Grant Heilman Photography; 3, 3A: Horticultural Photography, Corvallis, OR.; 4, 4A: Pamela Harper. 106, 1, 1A: Pamela Harper; 2, 2A, 3, 3A, 4, 4A: Michael Dirr. 107, 1, 1A: Michael Dirr; 2, 2A: Pamela Harper; 3, 3A: Thomas Eltzroth; 4, 4A: Michael Dirr. 108, 1: Runk/Schoenberger from Grant Heilman Photography; 1A: Grant Heilman Photography; 2, 2A, 3: Horticultural Photography, Corvallis, OR.; 3A, 4, 4A: Michael Dirr. 109, 1: Michael Dirr; 1A, Darrel Apps; 2: Pamela Harper; 2A: Michael Dirr; 3, 3A: Pamela Harper. 110, 1: Horticultural Photography, Corvallis, OR.; 1A: Pamela Harper; 2, 2A: Renée Comet; 3: John J. Smith/Photo-Nats; 3A: David Cavagnaro. 111, 1, 1A, 2, 2A: Horticultural Photography, Corvallis, OR.; 3, 3A: John J. Smith/Photo-Nats; 4: Paul Kingsley; 4A: Pamela Harper. 112, 1: Horticultural Photography, Corvallis, OR.; 1A, 2, 2A: Pamela Harper; 3, 3A, 4, 4A: Horticultural Photography, Corvallis, OR. 113, 1, 1A: Derek Fell; 2, 2A: Michael Dirr; 3, 3A, 4A: Pamela Harper; 4: Horticultural Photography, Corvallis, OR. 114, 1, 1A: Michael Dirr; 2, 2A: Steven Still; 3, 3A, 4: Michael Dirr; 4A: Pamela Harper. 115, 1, 1A, 2, 2A: Pamela Harper; 3: Grant Heilman Photography; 3A: Michael Dirr. 116, 1: Derek Fell; 1A: Al Bussewitz/Photo-Nats; 2, 2A: Steven Still; 3, 3A: Pamela Harper. 117, 1, 1A: Thomas Eltzroth; 2, 2A: Horticultural Photography, Corvallis, OR. 118, 1, 1A, 2, 3, 3A: Pamela Harper. 119, 1, 1A, 2A: Pamela Harper; 2: Horticultural Photography, Corvallis, OR.; 3, 3A: Michael Dirr. 120, 1: Horticultural Photography, Corvallis, OR.; 1A: Eugene Memmler; 2, 2A, 3A: Pamela Harper; 3: Steven Still. 121, 1: Derek Fell; 2, 2A: Michael Dirr; 3, 3A: Pamela Harper. 122, 1, 1A: Pamela Harper; 2, 2A: Michael Dirr; 3: Horticultural Photography, Corvallis, OR.; 3A: Al Bussewitz/Photo-Nats. 123, 1, 1A: Pamela Harper; 2, 2A, 3, 3A, 4: Horticultural Photography, Corvallis, OR.; 4A: Pamela Harper. 124, 1: Michael Dirr; 2, 3, 3A: Pamela Harper; 4: Michael Dirr; 4A, Julia MacKintosh. 125, 1: Al Bussewitz/Photo-Nats; 1A, 2, 3, 3A, 4: Pamela Harper. 126, 1: Steven Still; 1A: Michael Dirr; 2, 2A: Pamela Harper; 3, 3A: Horticultural Photography, Corvallis, OR. 127, 1, 1A: Horticultural Photography, Corvallis, OR.; 2, 2A, 3A: Michael Dirr; 3: Horticultural Photography, Corvallis, OR. 128, 1, 1A: Grant Heilman Photography; 2, 2A: Pamela Harper. 129, 1, 1A: Michael Dirr; 2: Horticultural Photography, Corvallis, OR.; 3, 3A: Darrel Apps. 130, 1: Horticultural Photography, Corvallis, OR.; 1A, 2: Pamela Harper; 2A: Michael Dirr. 131, 1, 1A: Bob Grant; 2: Runk/Schoenberger from Grant Heilman Photography; 3: Michael Dirr. 132, 1, 1A: Pamela Harper; 2, 2A, 3A: Michael Dirr; 3: Thomas Eltzroth. 133, 1, 1A: Michael Dirr; 2, 2A: Pamela Harper; 3, 3A, 4, 4A: Michael Dirr. 134, 1: Derek Fell; 2: Steven Still; 2A, 3: Pamela Harper; 3A: U.S. National Arboretum; 4, 4A: Michael Dirr. 135, 1, 1A, 2, 2A: Pamela Harper; 3, 3A: Bob Grant; 4, 4A: Pamela Harper. 136, 1, 1A, 2, 2A: Pamela Harper; 3: Michael Dirr; 4, 4A: Pamela Harper. 137, 1: Al Bussewitz/Photo-Nats; 1A: David Stone/Photo/Nats; 2: Michael Dirr; 3, 3A: Harrison L. Flint.

ACKNOWLEDGMENTS

The index for this book was prepared by Lynne R. Hobbs.
The editors also wish to thank: Wayne Ambler, Ashland, Virginia; Sarah Brash, Alexandria, Virginia; Sarah Broley, Washington, D.C.; Michael Dirr, University of Georgia, Athens, Georgia; George Good, Cornell University, Ithaca, New York; Matthew Grayson, Foxborough Nursery, Street, Maryland; Jimmy Groton, Knoxville, Tennessee; Kenneth E. Hancock, Annandale, Virginia; Mr. and Mrs. Victor J. Hernandes, Alexandria, Virginia; Edward Hasselfkus, University of Wisconsin, Madison, Wisconsin; Jon Hickey, North Massapequa, New York; Lee McKee, Washington, D.C.; Bernie Mihm, Fine Earth Landscaping, Poolesville, Maryland; Gary Moll, American Forestry Association, Washington, D.C.; Linda Morris, Baltimore, Maryland; Phil Normandy, Brookside Gardens, Wheaton, Maryland; Jayne E. Rohrich, Alexandria, Virginia; Candace H. Scott, College Park, Maryland; Floyd Swink, Morton Arboretum, Lisle, Illinois.

FURTHER READING

Bailey, Liberty Hyde, and Ethel Zoe Bailey, *Hortus Third: A Concise Dictionary of Plants Cultivated in the United States and Canada.* New York: Macmillan, 1976.

Brooklyn Botanic Garden, *Handbook on American Gardens: A Traveler's Guide.* Brooklyn, New York: Brooklyn Botanic Garden, 1986.

Brooklyn Botanic Garden, *Handbook on Flowering Trees.* Brooklyn, New York: Brooklyn Botanic Garden, 1986.

Davis, Brian, *The Gardener's Illustrated Encyclopedia of Trees & Shrubs.* Emmaus, Pennsylvania: Rodale Press, 1987.

Dirr, Michael A., *Manual of Woody Landscape Plants.* Champaign, Illinois: Stipes Publishing, 1983.

Dirr, Michael A., and Charles W. Heuser Jr., *The Reference Manual of Woody Plant Propagation.* Athens, Georgia: Varsity Press, 1987.

Edlin, Herbert L., *The Tree Key: A Guide to Identification in Garden, Field, and Forest.* New York: Scribner, 1978.

Fell, Derek, *Trees & Shrubs.* Tucson, Arizona: HP Books, 1986.

Ferguson, Barbara, ed., *All about Trees.* San Francisco: Ortho Books/Chevron Chemical Company, 1982.

Flint, Harrison L., *Landscape Plants for Eastern North America.* New York: John Wiley & Sons, 1983.

Forest Service, U.S. Department of Agriculture, *Seeds of Woody Plants in the United States.* (Agriculture Handbook No. 450.) Washington, D.C.: Forest Service, U.S. Department of Agriculture, 1974.

Haller, John M., *Tree Care.* New York: Macmillan, 1986.

Hill, Lewis, *Pruning Simplified.* Pownal, Vermont: Storey Communications, 1986.

Hill, Lewis, *Secrets of Plant Propagation.* Pownal, Vermont: Storey Communications, 1986.

The Hillier Colour Dictionary of Trees and Shrubs. North Pomfret, Vermont: David & Charles, 1984.

Krussman, Gerd, *Manual of Cultivated Broad-Leaved Trees and Shrubs.* 3 vols. Portland, Oregon: Timber Press, 1986.

Krussman, Gerd, *Manual of Cultivated Conifers.* Portland, Oregon: Timber Press, 1985.

Lanzara, Paola, and Mariella Pizzetti, *Guide to Trees.* New York: Simon and Schuster, 1978.

MacCaskey, Michael, ed., *Complete Guide to Basic Gardening.* Tucson, Arizona: HP Books, 1986.

Mitchell, Alan, *The Trees of North America.* New York: Facts on File, 1987.

National Audubon Society, *The Audubon Society Field Guide to North American Trees.* New York: Alfred A. Knopf, 1980.

Petrides, George A., *Trees and Shrubs.* Boston: Houghton Mifflin, 1986.

Phillips, Roger, *Trees of North America.* New York: Random House, 1978.

Rosendahl, Carl O., *Trees and Shrubs of the Upper Midwest.* Minneapolis: University of Minnesota Press, 1980.

Sinclair, Wayne A., Howard H. Lyon and Warren T. Johnson, *Diseases of Trees and Shrubs.* Ithaca, New York: Cornell University Press, 1987.

Smith, Ken, *Western Home Landscaping.* Tucson, Arizona: HP Books, 1978.

Smith, Michael D., ed., *The Ortho Problem Solver.* San Francisco: Ortho Books/Chevron Chemical Company, 1984.

Snyder, Leon C., *Trees and Shrubs for Northern Gardens.* Minneapolis: University of Minnesota Press, 1980.

Spangler, Ronald L., and Jerry Ripperda, *Landscape Plants for the Central and Northwestern United States.* Edina, Minnesota: Burgess International Group, 1977.

Wirth, Thomas, *The Victory Garden Landscape Guide.* Boston: Little, Brown, 1984.

Wyman, Donald, *Wyman's Gardening Encyclopedia,* New York: Macmillan, 1986.

INDEX

Time-Life Books Inc.
is a wholly owned subsidiary of

THE CONSULTANTS

C. Colston Burrell is the general consultant for The Time-Life Gardener's Guide. He is Curator of Plant Collections at the Minnesota Landscape Arboretum, part of the University of Minnesota, where he oversees plant collections and develops regional interest in the horticulture of the upper Midwest. Mr. Burrell is the author of publications about ferns and wildflowers, and a former curator of Native Plant Collections at the National Arboretum in Washington, D.C.

R. William Thomas, consultant for *Trees,* is a member of the staff of Longwood Gardens, an arboretum and plant conservatory near Wilmington, Delaware, where he directs visitor programs and teaches courses in ornamental plants. He is the author of numerous magazine articles on trees.

Library of Congress Cataloging-in-Publication Data
Trees.
    p.   cm.—(The Time-Life gardener's guide)
    Bibliography: p.
    Includes index.
    1. Ornamental trees.
I. Time-Life Books. II. Series.
SB435.T674 1988   635.9'77—dc19   88-12379   CIP
ISBN 0-8094-6616-3
ISBN 0-8094-66017-1 (lib. bdg.)

Time-Life Books Inc. offers a wide range of fine recordings, including a *Rock 'n' Roll Era* series. For subscription information, call 1-800-621-7026, or write Time-Life Music, P.O. Box C-32068, Richmond, Virginia 23261-2068.